D0882288

Are you baffled by why your company makes the same errors -- repeatedly? Would you like to focus your employees' limited time on more valuable work? Are you struggling to resolve an issue you know little about or make sense of overwhelming new responsibilities? The answer to all of these common challenges, and many more, is business process improvement (BPI).

The Power of Business Process Improvement: *The Workbook* simplifies the concepts presented in its hardcover counterpart. Susan Page provides the templates and tools to help you quickly move through the proven 10-step formula leading your business to become more effective, efficient, and adaptable.

Arranged in a results-oriented progression, the steps to BPI will help you:

- Eliminate bureaucracy.
- Explain what a process costs.
- Define process boundaries to reduce scope creep.
- Establish human controls to reduce human errors.
- Test and rework the process before introducing it to your business.
- Train and communicate the changes to your employees, customers, and stakeholders.
- Implement the change.

Use *The Workbook* individually or in a group setting to identify and prioritize the processes that need fixing, eliminate redundancy and bureaucracy, control costs, reduce errors, delight customers, and give your organization an edge on continuous improvement.

Take advantage of the online templates located on the author's web site www.susanpagebooks.com by using the special access code on page one.

The Power of

Business Process Improvement:

The WORKBOOK

Susan Page

Lowell Books
Jacksonville, FL

This publication is designed to provide accurate information, at the date of publication, in regard to the subject matter covered. It is sold with the understanding that the author or publisher is not engaged in rendering legal, accounting, or other professional service. If legal advice or other expert assistance is required, the services of a competent professional person should be sought.

The following are registered trademarks:
  Microsoft Office Access®
  Microsoft Office Excel®
  Microsoft Office Outlook®
  Microsoft Office PowerPoint®
  Microsoft Office Project®
  Microsoft Office SharePoint®
  Microsoft Office Suite®
  Microsoft Office Visio®

ISBN-13: 978-0-9760428-3-9
ISBN-10: 0-9760428-3-5

© 2013 Susan Page.
All rights reserved.
Printed in the United States of America.

This publication may not be reproduced, stored in a retrieval system, or transmitted in whole or in part, in any form or by any means, electronic, mechanical, photocopying, recording, or otherwise, without the prior written permission of the author, Susan Page, susan.page@cfl.rr.com.

Printing number
10 9 8 7 6 5 4 3 2 1

To Greg . . .

my inspiration

Contents

CHAPTER 10:
Step 10: *Drive Continuous Improvement*

CHAPTER 11:
Create the Executive Summary

CHAPTER 12:
Tools and Templates

The Power of

Business Process Improvement:

The WORKBOOK

Introduction

This workbook complements the book, The Power of Business Process Improvement, and provides a step-by-step guide to use as you facilitate a process improvement initiative. The hardcover book provides complete details and examples, while the workbook offers a streamlined approach to the ten steps and provides you with a tool you can use in a work team or class setting.

You will find each of the diagrams and forms used in the workbook included on the web site http://www.susanpagebooks.com. As a buyer of this workbook, you can download the forms and use them in your meetings and workshops as long as all documents retain the copyright information contained on each document. To access the secured section of the web site, simply enter the password "BPI731."

Facilitation

If you plan to work with a project team on business process improvement (BPI), begin a BPI session by identifying the goals of BPI:

- **Effectiveness**: Does the process produce the desired results and meet the customer's needs?
- **Efficiency**: Does the process minimize the use of resources and eliminate bureaucracy?
- **Adaptability**: Is the process flexible in the face of changing needs?

Stress the difference between effectiveness and efficiency and why effectiveness appears first because many people confuse the two terms. *Effectiveness* is all about the customer, while *efficiency* applies to the internal business. Since the customer is number one, always focus on effectiveness first.

Next, identify the ten steps to BPI so that the project team learns about the journey ahead. Select Figure 1, Figure 2, or Figure 3 to use in sharing the steps.

- **Figure 1** works well with a novice group because it looks like a road and does not appear threatening or complex.
- **Figure 2** works well with an experienced process team because it presents the steps in a flowchart, which this audience understands.
- **Figure 3** works for a management-level audience that you want to have awareness of the ten steps without the steps appearing too simple or too complex.

Choose the figure that helps your audience want to learn more about business process improvement and begin the journey.

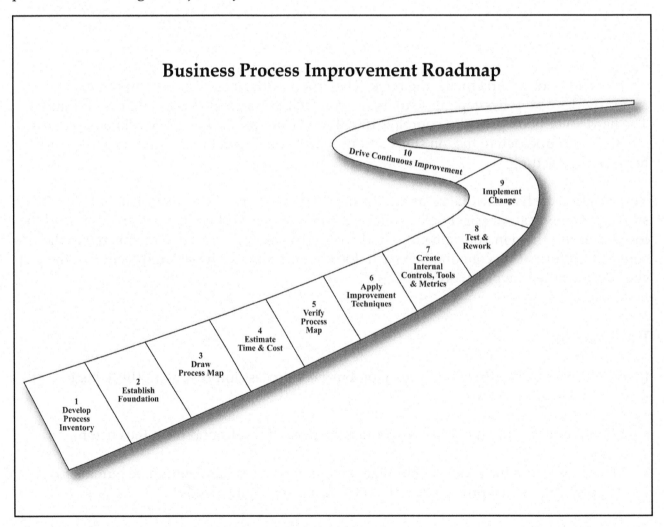

Figure 1: Business Process Improvement Roadmap

Business Process Improvement Flowchart

Objectives of Process Improvement:

- **Effectiveness**: does it produce the desired results and meet the customer's needs?
- **Efficiency**: does it minimize the use of resources and eliminate bureaucracy?
- **Adaptable**: is the process flexible to changing needs?

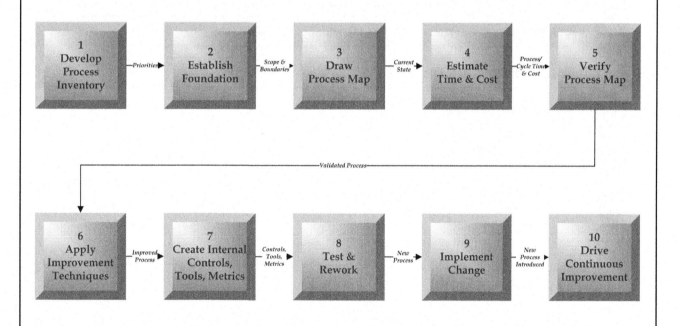

Gaining leadership buy-in and approval is ongoing throughout the process.

Figure 2: Business Process Improvement Flowchart

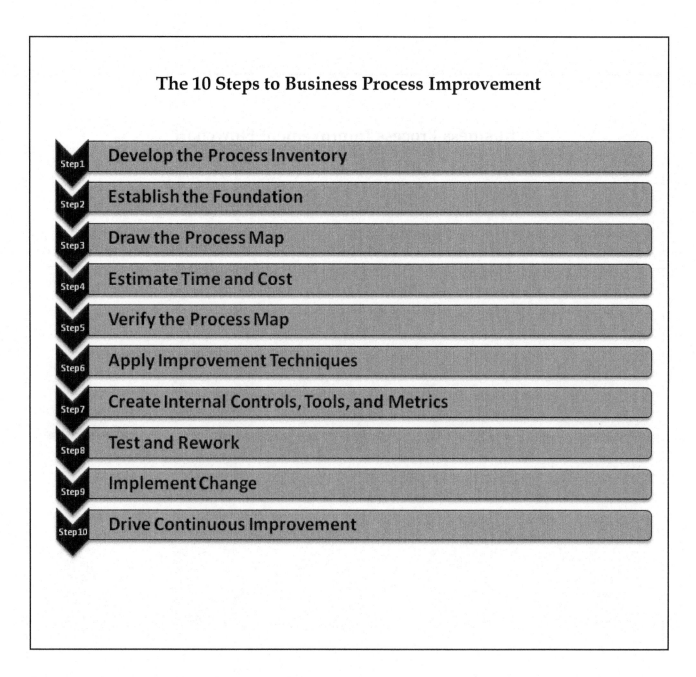

Figure 3: The 10 Steps to Business Process Improvement

CHAPTER 1

Step 1:

Develop the Process Inventory and Prioritize

OVERVIEW

When faced with multiple business processes in need of improvement, you have to identify which processes should rise to the top of the list to make certain that your organization focuses on the most important processes first.

This step helps you to build a process inventory and prioritize the list, so that you know where to focus your attention.

OUTCOMES

At the end of this step, you know where to focus your time because you developed:

- A process inventory
- Prioritization criteria
- Process prioritization matrix

1. Create the Process Inventory

The process inventory is a list of the business processes in an organization and it helps employees develop a common way to explain the business. Begin by deciding how to organize, or categorize, your business processes. You can organize business processes in different ways depending on your situation.

- **Cross functional**: prioritize business processes *across the organization* (e.g., across Finance, Sales & Marketing, Human Resources, Engineering, etc.)
- **Functional**: prioritize business processes *within a function* (e.g., in human resources, you might include the recruitment, compensation, and training processes)
- **Departmental**: prioritize business processes *within one department* (e.g., in the recruitment department, you might include sourcing, interviewing, and on boarding)

Figure 1-1 shows an example of organizing business processes by function and by department.

Human Resource Functions	Finance Department
Recruitment department » Requisition process » Sourcing process » Selection process » Orientation process **Compensation and benefits department** » Salary planning process » Job-leveling process » New hire pay process **Training department** » Need identification process » Course development process » Evaluation process	**Finance** » Budgeting » Forecasting » Payroll » Tax planning » Risk management » Cash management

Figure 1-1: Sample Categorization of Business Processes

To help build your inventory, think about the work and take the following into account:

- Review the work performed on a day-to-day basis
- Read employee job descriptions
- Look at organization charts
- Review department metrics
- Talk to employees

Exercise 1-1

Identify your business processes and who has overall responsibility for the process. If you use the cross functional method, enter the functions in the first column and use multiple rows in the *Business Process* column for each function's business processes. If you use the functional method, use the first column for the individual departments within the function and use multiple rows in the *Business Process* column for each department's business processes. If you use the departmental method, use the first column for the department name and list the department's business processes in the second column.

Categorization (Grouping) Method Used:

☐ Cross functional   ☐ Functional   ☐ Departmental

Function (or Department)	Business Process	Business Process Owner

Figure 1-2: Process Inventory

2. Identify Prioritization Criteria

Now that you have defined the organization's process inventory, you can decide what criteria to use to prioritize the list. The criteria help to determine which business process the organization should focus on first and contributes to a common understanding of what the organization deems important. Consider these four general categories and add custom criteria to each category that further helps to prioritize the business processes for your business:

1. **Impact**: how much does the business process affect your business?
    - Number affected by the business process
    - Customer or client level affected by the process
    - Custom criteria (add others as applicable)

2. **Implementation**: how feasible is it to make changes?
    - Time to market (consider the complexity of the process, potential delays, availability of knowledgeable resources)
    - Funding requirements (budget required to make changes)
    - Timing of next cycle (imminent, cyclical, six months away)
    - Custom criteria (add others as applicable)

3. **Current State**: how well is the process working today?
    - Customer satisfaction
    - Pain level to the internal business
    - Whether a process exists today or not
    - Custom criteria (add others as applicable)

4. **Value**: what is the benefit, or return, of improving the process?
    - Benefit
    - Return
    - Custom criteria (add others as applicable)

Exercise 1-2

Identify the prioritization criteria you will use to determine the priority of which business process to address first using Figure 1-3. Include custom categories and criteria applicable to your situation in the blank rows.

Categories	Criteria
IMPACT	▪ ▪ ▪ ▪
IMPLEMENTATION	▪ ▪ ▪ ▪
CURRENT STATE	▪ ▪ ▪ ▪
VALUE	▪ ▪ ▪ ▪
	▪ ▪ ▪ ▪
	▪ ▪ ▪ ▪
	▪ ▪ ▪ ▪

Figure 1-3: Prioritization Criteria

The next step before applying the criteria to the process inventory is to decide whether you want a criterion to carry more weight than another criterion.

DETERMINING WEIGHT

Decide whether you want to apply more weight to one of the categories, such as *value*. You may decide, for example, to apply the following weight:

- 35 percent for the impact category
- 10 percent for the implementation category
- 15 percent for the current state category
- 40 percent for the value category

Decide which is the most valuable category, then decide where each of the other categories fall with respect to that most valuable one: half as valuable, a third as valuable, and so forth. Assign weights so that the total of all categories equal 100, but do not feel that you must use weighting.

3. Develop the Process Prioritization Matrix

The prioritization matrix in Figure 1-4 brings together the process inventory and the prioritization criteria in one place to enable you to recognize where to start an improvement effort. Write the list of business processes identified in column one of the process prioritization matrix (process 1, process 2, process 3, etc.) and the prioritization criteria in the remaining columns of the matrix (impact, implementation, current state, etc.). Notice in Figure 1-4 that the prioritization sub-categories belong in row two.

Process	Impact			Implementation			Current State			Value			Total Score
Sub-category	# Affected	Level		Time to Market	Funding	Next Cycle							
Process 1													
Process 2													
Process 3													
Process 4													
Process 5													

Figure 1-4: Process Prioritization Matrix

Exercise 1-3

Complete Figure 1-5, 1-6, or 1-7 using your process inventory from Figure 1-2 and the prioritization criteria from Figure 1-3.

- Use Figure 1-5, if you do not plan to use weighting.
- Use Figure 1-6, if you want to use weighting. Assign a weight to each category on a scale of 1 to 100.
- Use Figure 1-7 to identify your own prioritization criteria.

In completing the process prioritization matrix, decide what scale you want to use. Consider whether to use a 1-3 scale, 1-5 scale, 1-10 scale, or something entirely different. Think about the scale so that when you total the score, the highest number tells you what process to work on first.

Sometimes you have to reverse the scale values, so that the total score tells the correct story. For example, let us assume that:

- *Number affected* (under impact) receives a **high** score because the number of employees affected by the business process is 100,000 employees. This high score will help move the business process towards the top of the priority list because it is more significant to have a large number of employees affected by a process. On a 1-5 scale, this would rate a 4 or 5.

- *Funding* (under implementation) receives a **low** score because no additional money is required to improve the business process. Because it is easier to improve a process if the effort does not require a budget, this is a positive circumstance. On a 1-5 scale, this would rate a 5. In this scenario, a low score receives the highest numerical value.

Process Prioritization Matrix

Process Name/Category	Impact		Implementation		Current State		Value		Total Score
Sub-category ↑									
1.									
2.									
3.									
4.									
5.									
6.									
7.									
8.									
9.									
10.									
11.									
12.									

Figure 1-5: Process Prioritization Matrix (no weighting)

Process Prioritization Matrix

Process Name/Category	Impact (%)		Implementation (%)		Current State (%)		Value (%)		Total Weighted Score
Sub-category ⟶		Sub-total/ Weight		Sub-total/ Weight		Sub-total/ Weight		Sub-total/ Weight	
1.									
2.									
3.									
4.									
5.									
6.									
7.									
8.									
9.									
10.									
11.									
12.									

Figure 1-6: Process Prioritization Matrix (with weighting)

Process Prioritization Matrix

Process Name/Category										Total Score
Sub-category ↑										
1.										
2.										
3.										
4.										
5.										
6.										
7.										
8.										
9.										
10.										
11.										
12.										

Figure 1-7: Process Prioritization Matrix

Summary

Building the process inventory organizes the business process work and it provides a tool to discuss the overall breadth of business processes. If you have a sponsor for your BPI work, he or she will probably add or subtract from the process inventory; so think of the inventory as a vehicle to encourage discussion between you and your sponsor.

After developing the business process inventory, identifying the prioritization categories, establishing criteria, developing a scale, and applying these items to each business process, you now have clear direction on where to start your improvement efforts. You can add more categories to the four general categories of impact, implementation, current state, and value or add prioritization criteria to meet your needs.

After applying the prioritization criteria to the process inventory, you have another occasion to discuss a meaningful topic with your sponsor. If the results do not reflect what the sponsor considers important, determine why your work and the sponsor's viewpoint seem disconnected, and decide whether you have to change the criteria, scale, or weighting. Validate that you and your sponsor agree on the priorities before beginning any process improvement work.

CHAPTER 2

Step 2:
Establish the Foundation

OVERVIEW

Once you select a business process to improve, the next step is to build the foundation for the improvement effort – your *blueprint*.

This step helps you to develop a common understanding with the project team of a business process, clarify terminology, establish boundaries to help you avoid scope creep, identify customers and their needs, and define success.

This is the most important step of the ten steps to business process improvement and you should *never* skip this step.

OUTCOMES

At the end of this step, you have a basic understanding of the business process you intend to focus on, you know your scope, and you have agreements because you:

- Developed a scope definition document
- Gained buy-in from the project sponsor

1. Create the Scope Definition Document

The Scope Definition Document (SDD), or foundation, helps to establish baseline information about a specific business process. It becomes your blueprint.

After building the process inventory and identifying where to begin, this document helps to keep the work on track as you move through the improvement steps on a single business process. It keeps the project team on track by clarifying the scope of work and helps you to avoid scope creep.

The keys to creating a successful SDD include:

- Completing it with the project team.
- Remaining flexible throughout its creation, making changes as necessary.
- Documenting unique terminology used in the SDD.
- Keeping the SDD to a single page for quick reference.
- Adapting the SDD, by adding or deleting sections, as your situation requires.

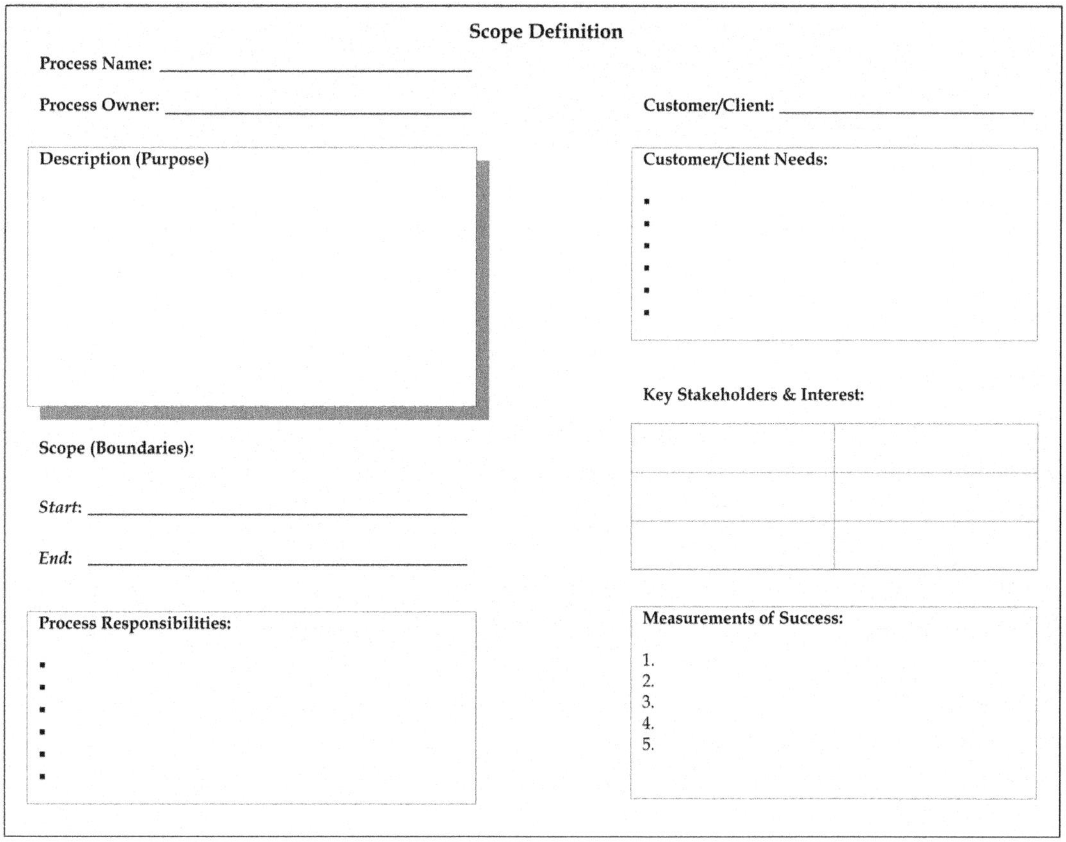

Scope Definition

Process Name: ______

Process Owner: ______

Customer/Client: ______

Description (Purpose)

Customer/Client Needs:

-
-
-
-
-
-

Key Stakeholders & Interest:

Scope (Boundaries):

Start: ______

End: ______

Process Responsibilities:

-
-
-
-
-
-

Measurements of Success:

1.
2.
3.
4.
5.

Figure 2-1: Scope Definition Document

The SDD in Figure 2-1 has eight sections.

SECTION 1: PROCESS NAME

Identify the name of the business process, such as the *hiring process*, the *budget process*, or the *software development process*.

Figure 2-2: Process Name

SECTION 2: PROCESS OWNER

Identify the *one* person who has ultimate responsibility for the process even if the process touches multiple departments. Think of who has budgetary authority or who has to answer to senior management if something goes wrong.

Figure 2-3: Process Owner

SECTION 3: DESCRIPTION (PURPOSE)

When completing this section, think about how to explain the business process to a new employee or someone unfamiliar with the process. Think of the following as you write the description:

- Use simple terminology, not specific to the process.
- Avoid the use of technical terms – if you feel that you must use a technical term, explain what it means by using footnotes.
- Identify anything out of scope (e.g., This process does <u>not</u> cover the following types of reimbursement: *then list the types*).
- Provide examples if necessary (e.g., "eligible" claims include: *then list the types of eligible claims*).

The description alone can easily take an hour to complete, and it is worth every minute.

DESCRIPTION (PURPOSE)

Figure 2-4: Description (Purpose)

SECTION 4: SCOPE (BOUNDARIES)

The scope identifies the breadth or area covered by the business process and establishes the boundaries within which you will perform the improvement work. This section helps you to stay on track as you progress deeper into the work.

Identify the *start* and *end* point of the business process. There is no right or wrong answer. For example, in the hiring process you can define the start as "approval for head count," or begin with "sourcing candidates," or pick another starting point. Make certain that everyone agrees with the start of the process or you will find yourself revisiting it later.

PROCESS START	PROCESS END

Figure 2-5: Scope (Boundaries)

SECTION 5: PROCESS RESPONSIBILITIES

This is a list of the major tasks that the business process must deliver, and it provides you with an opportunity to validate the *description* and *scope* sections of the scope definition document.

Responsibilities, for example, for the *hiring* process can include items such as sourcing, pre-screening, interviewing, and background checks, among other tasks.

If you list a responsibility in section 5, not supported by either the description or the scope, stop and revisit your earlier work. While it may seem time consuming to stop, you will find it easier to correct it here rather than later when you are well into the work.

Identify the top five (5) tasks that the business process has responsibility to deliver.

PROCESS RESPONSIBILITIES
1.
2.
3.
4.
5.

Figure 2-6: Process Responsibilities

SECTION 6: CUSTOMER (CLIENT) AND NEEDS

In this section, think about the customer (or internal client) and what is important to them from the business process.

Identify the customer/client of the process and list their needs.

CUSTOMER (CLIENT)	CUSTOMER (CLIENT) NEEDS

Figure 2-7: Customer/Client and Needs

SECTION 7: KEY STAKEHOLDERS AND INTEREST

Now think about the key stakeholders of the process and what is important to them from the business process. Although the customer is the main focus of business process improvement work, other areas or departments can either affect a business process or receive the downstream effect of a business process.

Identify the key stakeholders of the process and identify their area(s) of interest.

KEY STAKEHOLDER	AREA(S) OF INTEREST

Figure 2-8: Key Stakeholders and Areas of Interest

SECTION 8: MEASUREMENTS OF SUCCESS

This section helps you think about what you want to measure.

Looking back at what you identified as customer and stakeholder needs, identify how you will know if the business process successfully meets those needs. In addition to this type of effectiveness measurement, you can include internal metrics that help increase the efficiency and adaptability of the business.

At this point, do not think about *how* to conduct a measurement, just identify *what* you want to measure.

MEASUREMENTS OF SUCCESS
1.
2.
3.
4.
5.

Figure 2-9: Measurements of Success

Combine all eight sections into a one-page document, like the one in Figure 2-1, to make it easy to read. Consider it a quick reference tool. Keeping the scope definition document to a single sheet of paper helps all employees easily scan it for information.

Complete a scope definition document *before* beginning any improvement effort because it helps to ground everyone involved in the business process improvement work and ensures that all participants have the same level of understanding. Complete this document jointly with the project team.

Exercise 2-1

Complete Figure 2-10 for the business process you identified as your top priority in step 1.

2. Gain Buy-in

Review the completed scope definition document with the business process improvement sponsor, and adjust it as necessary. Revisit the changed document (if applicable) with the project team to ensure that everyone agrees with the changes that the sponsor made to the SDD. Once all agree, consider the scope "locked" and do not veer off course without a good reason and without renegotiating the time and resources to do the work. The SDD is now your blueprint.

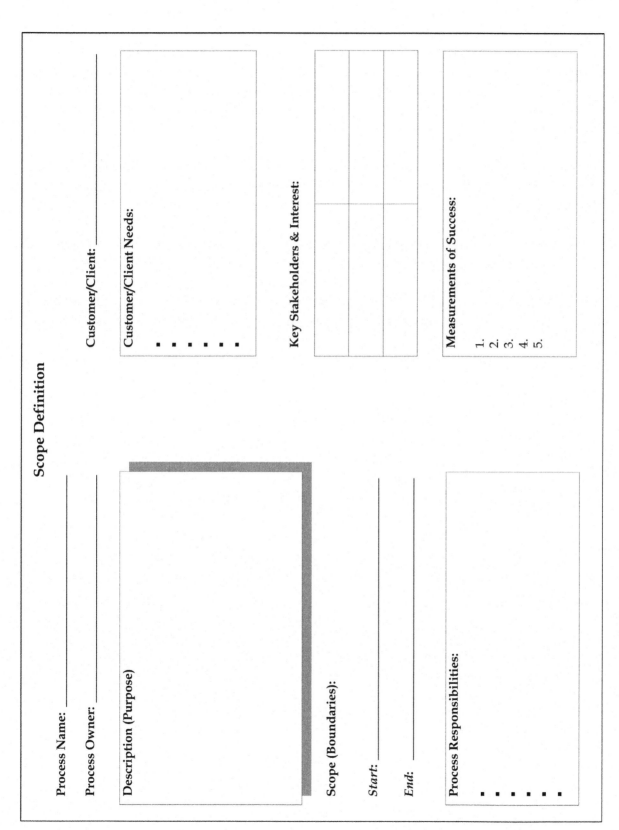

Figure 2–10: Scope Definition Document

Summary

Discussing this baseline information with the project team at the start of the first meeting allows everyone to have input and assists the team in creating a common understanding of the terminology and business process. As you develop the scope definition document, remain flexible so that in the end you feel comfortable that everyone has had a chance to provide input to the scope of the work and that everyone understands what is, and is not, included in the business process.

Once the team has agreed on the content of the SDD, review it with the sponsor (if applicable) and gain approval. The sponsor will appreciate the conciseness of the document, so keep it to a single piece of paper.

The scope definition document works like a contract, one that you can revisit, as needed, to reinforce the agreements made. You should consider it "locked" to a certain extent.

You should feel free to change the scope definition document template to fit your needs. Take components out and put others in to address any specific situations you may encounter. The document is meant to be flexible.

Note

Chapter 9 discusses the requirements for a project plan to guide the work. You can stop at any point and review that chapter, but continuing with the ten steps will provide you with a greater understanding of what each step entails and allow you to develop a better project plan.

CHAPTER 3

Step 3:
Draw the Process Map

OVERVIEW

Drawing a process map enables everyone in the organization to understand how a business process works and where handoffs occur between departments. It gives all employees involved in the work a common understanding of how the process works by educating them on the end-to-end process.

This step provides the baseline information you require to identify the amount of time a process requires today and determine the process cost. The step also assists in setting improvement targets when you move to the improvement step.

OUTCOMES

At the end of this step, you and the project team have a common understanding of the end-to-end business process because you have:

- Created a process map
- Documented the steps involved in the business process

1. Process Mapping Basics

DEFINITION: A process map is a visual representation of a series of connected activities that deliver a meaningful outcome to a customer.

PROCESS MAPPING SYMBOLS

While many process map symbols exist, you will find five that you use on a regular basis. Figure 3-1 shows the most common symbols.

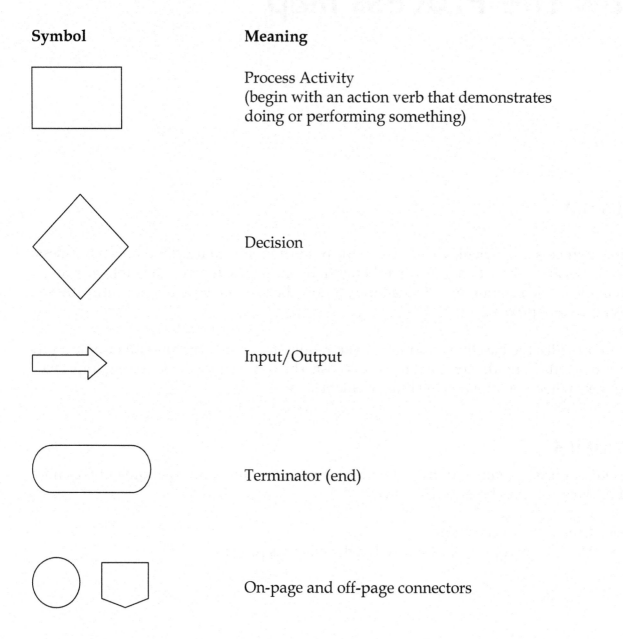

Symbol	Meaning
	Process Activity (begin with an action verb that demonstrates doing or performing something)
	Decision
	Input/Output
	Terminator (end)
	On-page and off-page connectors

Figure 3-1 Common Process Mapping Symbols

PROCESS MAPPING FLOW

Figure 3-2 depicts the normal process map flow. The arrow in Figure 3-2 shows that the *output* from the first activity, becomes the *input* for the second activity.

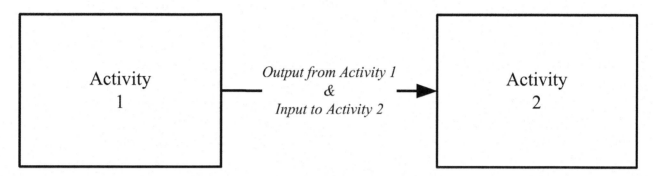

Figure 3-2 Normal Process Map Flow

Figure 3-3 shows an example where activity 1 states "Run Turnover Report," and the output identifies what information results from running the report. Activity 2 explains what to do with that information. In this example, the business process (in activity 2) calls for an employee to analyze the trends from the monthly turnover numbers.

Figure 3-3 Sample Process Map Flow

LEVEL OF DETAIL FOR PROCESS MAPS

You can decide to draw a process map at a *high* level, at a *detailed* level, or somewhere in between. You base this decision on what you require to achieve your goals. Figure 3-4 provides criteria to help you decide at what level to draw a process map.

Even if you start at a high level, you can always add more details later if the need surfaces.

DETAILED LEVEL	HIGH LEVEL
Draw a detailed-level process map if the process: ■ Is used often by many people. ■ Experiences high turnover among process workers. ■ Is a subprocess of another business process.	Draw a high-level process map if the process: ■ Is undefined and little shared understanding exists in the organization of the end-to-end business process. ■ Is a complex process. ■ Is a highly variable process. ■ Has many subprocesses.

Figure 3-4 Determining the Level of Process Map

2. Draw the Process Map

Often, the most difficult step in drawing a process map is getting started. To make this step easier, refer to the scope definition document, created in step 2, and review the *scope* that you identified in section four of the document. Figure 3-5 shows the format for the beginning of a process map using a recruiting example, where the process starts with extending a job offer to a candidate.

1. **Activity**: Use the information that states where the process *starts* as the beginning point for the process map and enter this information in the activity 1 box. Start with an action verb. Number the process box for each activity as you go.

2. **Output**: Enter the output of activity 1 on the right-facing arrow leaving the box. Remember that activity 2 must use what you identify as the output. If you cannot use the result of activity 1 in activity 2, then rewrite activity 1.

3. **Responsible Party**: Identify the employee who performs the activity by writing the job title below the activity box. In Figure 3-5, the recruiter has responsibility for extending the job offer to the selected candidate. In some organizations, the hiring manager may extend the offer, so identifying the responsible party adds clarity to the business process.

4. **Annotation**: Add annotations as you move through the process map to capture critical notes directly on the process map so that they remain visible.

5. **Tools**: Add symbols to denote the system, form, or other tools used at each step in the business process.

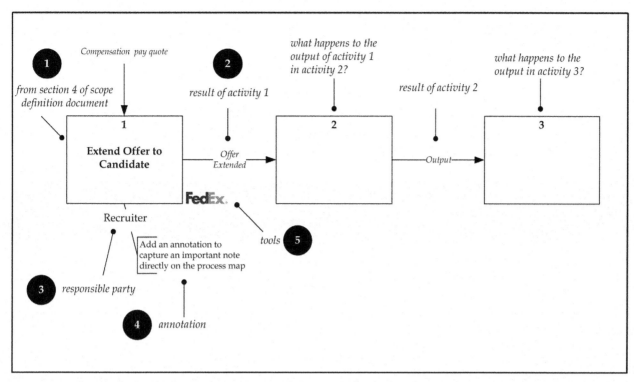

Figure 3-5 Sample Process Map

ALTERNATIVE PROCESS MAP

You may find it helpful to use a *cross-functional* process map, where a horizontal section is designated for each functional area. This alternative shows the relationship and dependency between functional areas. You can draw this type of process map either horizontal or vertical. Figure 3-6 shows a horizontal cross-functional process map.

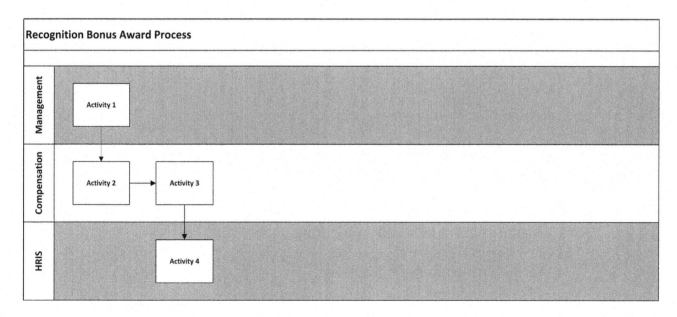

Figure 3-6 Cross-functional Process Map (horizontal)

3. Develop Detail Document

As you build the process map, create the detail document at the same time. This narrative description should accompany the process map because it enables employees to choose either a graphical or textual representation of the process, depending on their personal preference. Figure 3-7 shows the components to include in the detail document and Figure 3-8 provides a completed example using the recruiting scenario from Figure 3-5.

ACTIVITY NUMBER	ACTIVITY NAME AND DESCRIPTION	INPUT/OUTPUT	TOOLS USED
1	Title and narrative description	Input: Output:	List tools

Figure 3-7 Detail Document Template

ACTIVITY NUMBER	ACTIVITY NAME AND DESCRIPTION	INPUT/OUTPUT	TOOLS USED
1	**EXTEND OFFER TO CANDIDATE** The recruiter extends a written offer to the candidate. The offer includes a total reward statement that shows the candidate the value of all benefits, beyond just the rate of pay offered.	Input: Compensation quote Output: Offer extended	Offer package is sent via Federal Express

Figure 3-8 Example of Detail Document

Exercise 3-1

Use Figure 3-9 to draw a process map for the business process you identified in Figure 2-10, following these five steps:

1. Add activities
2. Identify output (and associated input to the next activity)
3. List responsible party
4. Include annotations, if necessary
5. Identify tools used

Use Figure 3-10 to create the detail document to complement the process map.

Process Name _____

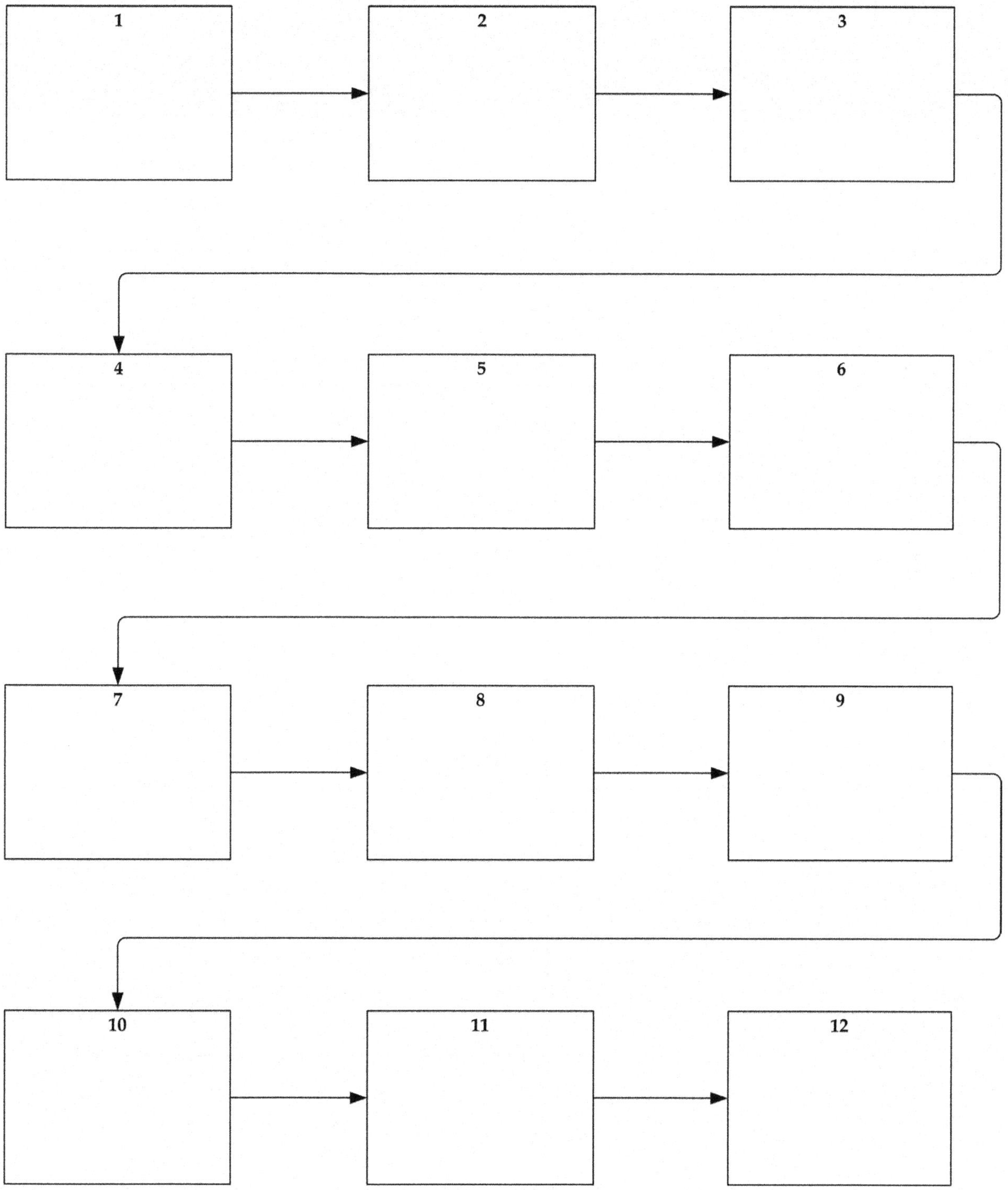

Figure 3-9 Process Map Template

Process Name _____

ACTIVITY NUMBER	ACTIVITY NAME AND DESCRIPTION	INPUT/OUTPUT	TOOLS USED
1			
2			
3			
4			
5			
6			
7			
8			
9			

Figure 3-10 Detail Document

Activity Number	Activity Name and Description	Input/Output	Tools Used
10			
11			
12			

4. Continuing the Work from Meeting to Meeting

More often than not, you will find it difficult to complete a process map in one meeting unless the work encompasses a simple business process or you plan a long meeting. Since everyone involved in helping to draw the process map returns to their normal jobs once the meeting ends, you will find that not too many people remember the details of the process map the project team started creating when they come back together at the next meeting. As a result, you have to accomplish several tasks between meetings, to help jump-start the team's memory at the next meeting:

1. Create/refine the process map using Microsoft Visio or other business process software.
2. Write the detail document.
3. Enlarge the process map.
4. Make copies of the process map and detail document.

At the beginning of the next meeting, hang the enlarged process map on the wall and start the meeting by walking the team through the partially completed process map to remind everyone of what they accomplished at the first meeting. Walk through the process map activity by activity, highlighting what occurs at each step, naming the responsible party, explaining any annotations, and identifying the tools used. Physically point to different sections on the process map, explain the output of each activity, and describe how the output is used in the next step of the process.

You should allow and encourage the project team to stop and change the process map as you walk through it because it is the first time that they see the map in its clean state. Stop every time someone has a question and discuss the issue. If anyone has a question, it means something on the process map probably has to change. Write any changes directly on the enlarged process map using a thick marker so that everyone can see the map changing.

After you finish reviewing the enlarged process map hanging on the wall, switch back to the board or easel and continue drawing the next steps in the process. Ideally, you can use an electronic, dry-erase board.

Summary

Drawing the process map helps everyone involved better understand how the business process works, where handoffs occur between departments, and it provides the background needed to apply the improvement techniques described in step 6.

Creating the design document supports the process map and provides additional information about the process. It also allows employees to choose how they prefer to review the material.

CHAPTER 4

Step 4:
Estimate Time and Cost

OVERVIEW

After drawing the process map, you understand the activities involved in a business process and step 4 helps you to identify how *long* the process takes to complete from beginning to end, how much *labor* the process uses, and what the process *costs*. In a later step, you can use this information to set improvement targets.

While you may decide to use formal methods to calculate the process time, estimating usually works well in an administrative environment because employees generally have a good idea of how long a task takes to complete.

Collect the process and cycle time *last*, after you finished drawing the process map, so that you have a clear understanding of the steps involved in the business process.

OUTCOMES

At the end of this step, you know how long the business process takes and what it costs because you:

- Defined process and cycle time
- Calculated the labor cost

1. Process and Cycle Time

You often hear two types of time related to business processes: *process* and *cycle* time.

DEFINITION:

- **Process time**: the time required to complete a single activity in a process.
- **Cycle time**: the time required to complete an entire process, from the first step to the last step in a process. Sometimes, you hear this referred to as elapsed time.

Process Time

In order to establish an improvement target, you first have to define the *baseline*, how long the process takes today. Without a baseline, you cannot establish an improvement target.

DEFINITION: A baseline is a line serving as a basis, as for measurement, calculation, or location.

To identify the process time, walk through the process map developed in step 3 and identify the amount of time required for each activity. Add this information to the process map above each activity process box in the left-hand corner. Figure 4-1 shows the placement of this information.

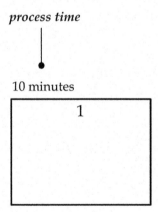

Figure 4-1 Example of Where to Show Process Time

If employees feel more comfortable providing a range, simply note the range on the process map (e.g., 10-15 minutes). Later you will use the mid-point of the range to perform calculations.

Figure 4-2 shows a table you can create after collecting the process time information on the process map. In this example, processing one transaction, which includes eight activities, requires approximately one hour of labor (using the mid-point between the *low* and *high* end time estimates).

ACTIVITY NUMBER	LOW END	HIGH END
1	10 minutes	15 minutes
2	5 minutes	7 minutes
3	5 minutes	5 minutes
4	n/a	n/a
5	15 minutes	20 minutes
6	5 minutes	5 minutes
7	5 minutes	5 minutes
8	10 minutes	12 minutes
Total	**55 minutes**	**69 minutes**

Figure 4-2 Example of Process Time Summary

Cycle Time

Customers frequently notice how long an entire process takes and if you define a measurement of success as reducing cycle time, collecting cycle time information will help you know whether or not you succeed in meeting this success measurement.

To accomplish this task, walk through the process map and identify the waiting time between each activity. Add this information to the process map above each activity process box in the right-hand corner. Figure 4-3 shows the placement of this information.

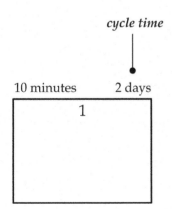

Figure 4-3 Example of Where to Show Cycle Time

Figure 4-4 shows a table you can create once you collect the cycle time information to show how long the end-to-end process takes. In this example, processing one complete cycle requires approximately 16.4 days.

ACTIVITY NUMBER	NUMBER OF HOURS	NUMBER OF DAYS
1	1 hour	.125 days
2	40 hours	5 days
3	32 hours	4 days
4	n/a	n/a
5	2 hours	.25 days
6	40 hours	5 days
7	8 hours	1 day
8	8 hours	1 day
Total	**131 hours**	**16.4 days**

Figure 4-4 Example of Cycle Time Summary

Exercise 4-1

Revisit Figure 3-9 and add the *process* and *cycle* time for each activity directly on the process map.

To prepare for calculating the labor cost for the business process, transfer the low and high end process times from Figure 3-9 to Figure 4-5. Calculate the average time (the mid-point) and use the "average process time" column to write this value.

For example, the average process time in Figure 4-2 for activity number 5 is 17.5 minutes (the mid-point between 15 minutes and 20 minutes).

Process Name _____

ACTIVITY NUMBER	DESCRIPTION	LOW END	HIGH END	AVERAGE PROCESS TIME
1				
2				
3				
4				
5				
6				
7				
8				
9				
10				
11				
12				
Total				

Figure 4-5 Process Time Summary

2. Calculating Labor Cost

To estimate the labor cost of a business process, follow these four (4) points:

1. Use a spreadsheet to list the process activities and average process times.
2. Identify the annual volume.
3. Determine the FTE (full-time equivalent) number to use, which identifies the number of employees required to support the business process.
4. Determine the salary and employee benefit rate to use for the employees involved in the process.

Note

Before proceeding with this calculation, you may want to perform the validation identified in step 5 to confirm that all parties agree with the process map activities and time estimates. This may save you time if you receive pushback on your estimates.

PART 1: PROCESS ACTIVITIES AND TIMES

Figure 4-5 summarized the process information. You can use that figure if you want to look at the entire business process regardless of departments involved.

If you want to focus on the labor used by a specific department, use Figure 4-6 instead. Revisit Figure 3-9 to identify the responsible employee who performs an activity and translate the information to a department name. Use that information to populate the *department* columns in Figure 4-6.

Exercise 4-2

Complete Figure 4-6 if you want to analyze the labor consumed by departments. Include as many departments as necessary by adding more columns.

Figure 4-6 will show the total time required for the business process (total average process time) and the individual process time required by department for those areas involved in delivering the process outcomes.

Skip this exercise if you do not want to identify labor by department.

ACTIVITY NUMBER	DESCRIPTION	AVERAGE PROCESS TIME	DEPARTMENT 1 TIME	DEPARTMENT 2 TIME
1				
2				
3				
4				
5				
6				
7				
8				
9				
10				
11				
12				
Total minutes/transaction (Total hours/transaction)				

Figure 4-6 Process Summary by Department

PART 2: ANNUAL VOLUME

Identify how many transactions the organization handles on an annual basis (e.g., the number of reimbursements, hires, compensation awards, etc.). Use the formula in Figure 4-7 to calculate how many labor hours the process consumes.

> **Annual Volume x Minutes (or Hours) per Transaction =**
> **Total Annual Minutes (or Hours)**

Figure 4-7 Formula for Annual Process Time

Continuing with the example from Figure 4-2, which requires an average of 62 minutes of labor per transaction, and assuming that the business handles 2,500 transactions per year, Figure 4-8 shows that the business process in question uses 2,575 hours of labor a year to handle the current volume of transactions.

> **2,500 x 62 minutes per transaction = 155,000 Annual Minutes**
> (155,000/60 minutes per hour = 2,583 hours)
> or
> **2,500 x 1.033 hours per transaction = 2,583 Annual Hours**

Figure 4-8 Example of Annual Process Time

Exercise 4-3

Calculate the annual hours consumed by your business process in Figure 4-5 or Figure 4-6 by using the work area in Figure 4-9.

Annual volume	
Hours per transaction *	X
Total Annual Hours	=

* Translate minutes to hours by dividing the number of minutes by 60 (60 minutes per hour)

Figure 4-9 Annual Process Labor

PART 3: FTE FORMULA

The term *FTE* (*full-time equivalent*) is used to account for percentages of an employee's time spent on a business process. Assuming that an employee works 40 hours in a week, FTE equates to 2,080 hours in a year (40 hours a week x 52 weeks a year). Very few employees work this amount of hours though in a year because of benefits like vacation, holiday, and sick pay. Remove this type of pay to determine the FTE calculation to use at your company.

Figure 4-10 shows an example of the formula to use for determining the FTE. This example shows 1,880 as the standard working hours per employee (instead of 2,080).

FTE Calculation Used: 1,880

Annual hours	2,080*
Less 2 weeks vacation	80
Less 1 week sick	40
Less 10 days paid holidays	80
Total	**1,880**

*40 hours per week x 52 weeks in a year

Figure 4-10 Example of FTE Calculation

This step translates the annual hours spent on the business process into the number of employees those hours represent, using the FTE concept. For example, Figure 4-8 showed that the business process required 2,583 annual hours of labor, and if you divide that number by the "FTE calculation used" number in Figure 4-10, you can see that the business process requires 1.37 FTEs, or one and one-third employees, to do the work (2,583 hours in Figure 4-8 divided by 1,880 hours in Figure 4-10).

Exercise 4-4

Determine the FTE number you plan to use by completing the formula in Figure 4-11. Add other deductions if you want to exclude additional types of working hours (besides vacation, sick, and holiday).

Annual hours		2,080
Less vacation time allowed	-	hrs.
Less sick time allowed	-	hrs.
Less paid holidays	-	hrs.
Less other	-	hrs.
Less other	-	hrs.
FTE Calculation to Use	=	

Figure 4-11 FTE Calculation

Now that you know the FTE number to use, you can combine this information with the total annual hours from Figure 4-9 to identify the number of FTEs required to deliver the process outcome. You will use this number to determine the process cost.

Exercise 4-5

Complete the formula in Figure 4-12 to identify the FTE labor used by your business process.

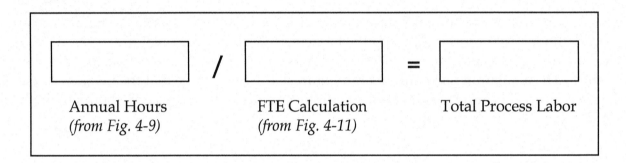

Annual Hours
(from Fig. 4-9)

FTE Calculation
(from Fig. 4-11)

Total Process Labor

Figure 4-12 FTEs Used by Business Process

PART 4: EMPLOYEE SALARY AND BENEFIT RATE

The final step involves bringing in the salary of the employees involved in the process work. For simplicity sake, assume that the 1.37 FTEs in the earlier example each earn $50,000 a year. The business process appears to cost the organization $68,500 in labor costs (50,000 x 1.37 FTE).

However, the Employee Benefit rate (or EB rate) is still missing. Employees cost more than just their salary, and the EB rate used by an organization adds their company-sponsored benefits to the employee's salary to come up with a total employee cost. For this example, we will use a 30% EB rate. Figure 4-13 shows the formula for determining total employee cost and Figure 4-14 shows an example.

Employee labor cost x (100% + 30% EB rate) =
Total Employee Cost dedicated to business process

Figure 4-13 Formula for Total Employee Cost

$$\$68,500 \times 130\% = \$89,050$$

Figure 4-14 Example of Total Employee Cost

Exercise 4-6

Calculate the labor cost of your business process by completing the formula in Figure 4-15.

- Obtain the annual salary from your compensation department for the affected employees. If you have multiple departments, repeat this calculation as often as necessary.
- Obtain your company's Employee Benefit rate from your finance department.

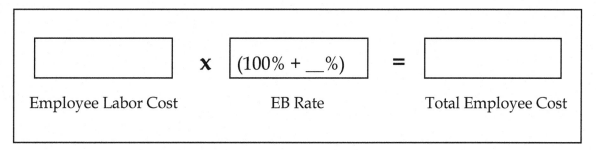

| Employee Labor Cost | **x** | (100% + __%) | **=** | Total Employee Cost |

Figure 4-15 Labor Cost of Business Process

Labor Cost Summary

After completing the four steps to calculating the labor cost, you know the following about the business process:

1. Each transaction consumes _____ hours
2. Annual volume is _____
3. Requires _____ FTE(s)
4. The process costs $_____ in labor

From here, you can include additional costs like system resources or overhead costs. You can also cut the data in various ways to show *cost per transaction* or *most expensive activity.*

You may have different types of employees involved in the business process, as depicted in your process map, so include all types that apply because they each have a different rate of pay. Figure 4-16 shows the type of spreadsheet you should create to summarize this information. This figure shows a training and development example.

EMPLOYEE TYPE	PROCESS TIME/ ACTIVITY	ANNUAL VOLUME	ANNUAL LABOR	FTE *
Instructional designer	180.0 hours	30	5,400 hours	2.9
Evaluation specialist	34.0 hours	30	1,020 hours	0.5
Instructor	9.5 hours	1,000	9,500 hours	5.1
Learning consultant	10.0 hours	130	1,300 hours	0.7
Enrollment specialist	0.28 hours	25,000	7,000 hours	3.7
Total FTEs required				**12.9**

* Using 1,880 FTE calculation

Figure 4-16   Example of Labor Estimate for Training and Development

In this example, you see that 12.9 employees are involved in the process, but they do not earn the same salary. Add two additional columns to Figure 4-16 (*Average Salary* and *Cost by Employee Type*) to show the complete labor picture. Figure 4-17 provides a blank template to record this information.

Exercise 4-7

Complete Figure 4-17 for your business process to identify the total *labor* cost of the business process.

Labor Calculation

Process Name: _____

EMPLOYEE TYPE	PROCESS TIME/ ACTIVITY (HOURS)	ANNUAL VOLUME	ANNUAL LABOR (HOURS)	FTE	AVERAGE SALARY	COST BY EMPLOYEE TYPE
TOTAL						

Figure 4-17 Labor Cost for Business Process

3. Tools and Overhead

In addition to labor costs you may want to add the cost of *tools* used by the employees to deliver the process outcome and *overhead* costs.

DEFINITION: Overhead refers to the ongoing expenses associated with running a business and includes things like the physical office space an employee occupies, utilities, supplies, taxes, insurance, and computer equipment. You may find that your company considers all administrative business processes as overhead because they do not deliver a product sold to customers.

A 150 percent overhead rate, for example, means that for each $1.00 of direct labor, an additional $1.50 is added for overhead costs. To calculate the overhead rate, divide overhead costs by direct (e.g., labor) costs.

Exercise 4-8

Complete Figure 4-18 for your business process to include all costs associated with the business process.

- Allocate the appropriate portion of software costs, for example, by employee type to define *tool* costs.
- Use your company's *overhead rate* for overhead costs.

4. Summary

Identifying the labor, tool, and overhead costs associated with a business process brings a financial component to your work and helps you to explain how processes and costs relate to each other. The full-time equivalent (FTE) formula identifies the percentage of employee time spent supporting a business process. Learning to apply the employee benefit and overhead rate gives you a perspective of the total employee cost.

After completing the calculations described in this chapter, you can cut the data numerous ways to meet your needs, including:

- The cost for each step in the process.
- The cost per transaction.
- The time from beginning to end.
- Where to focus your time in the improvement stage.
- Other statistics that you want to share.

Total Process Cost

Process Name: _____

Employee Type	Process Time/ Activity (Hours)	Annual Volume	Labor Cost		Tool Cost	Overhead Cost	Total Cost
TOTAL							

Figure 4-18 Total Costs for Business Process

CHAPTER 5

Step 5:

Verify the Process Map

OVERVIEW

After completing the process map, review it with interested parties to confirm that it accurately reflects the existing process *before* moving to the improvement step. At a minimum, include the sponsor, process workers, and stakeholders in the review process.

As you review the process map with the process workers, make certain that you confirm the time estimates since you will use this information to establish the process cost.

This step may happen fast or it may take weeks depending on the number of people that have to review the process map.

OUTCOMES

At the end of this step, you have buy-in that you accurately documented the business process, which helps you to avoid challenges regarding the improvement targets (or actual improvements) later on, after you have applied the improvement techniques. You have gained:

- Agreement on the validity of the process map and time estimates
- Buy-in from the sponsor on your financial evaluation

1. Interested Parties

Validating the process map, before moving to the improvement phase, enables interested parties to provide input on the:

- Accuracy of the process map
- Points requiring clarification
- Estimates for process and cycle times

Sponsor

Before walking the sponsor through the process map, review the scope definition document you created in step 2 with him or her. Highlight the boundaries from that document as a transition to the entry point on the process map, and then walk the sponsor through the entire process map highlighting inputs and outputs, time estimates, and other key points. You should personally conduct the review with the sponsor.

Process Workers

Include process workers responsible for the various activities in the process map. Use the scope definition document to help identify whom to include in the review. If a process worker has ownership for delivering on the process responsibilities identified, include that individual in the validation step. Assign the project team responsibility to validate the information because it helps to engage the team in the work and increases their sense of ownership.

Exercise 5-1

Use Figure 5-1 to identify the process workers that you plan to include in the validation step. Include the process worker's name, his or her department, when the meeting with the process worker will occur, and the project team member responsible for conducting the verification. Sequence the meetings in a logical flow.

Process Worker Validation

EMPLOYEE NAME	DEPARTMENT	TIMEFRAME	RESPONSIBLE PARTY

Figure 5-1 Process Worker Validation

STAKEHOLDERS

Identify appropriate stakeholders to include in the verification based on what you said the stakeholders care about in the scope definition document. Meet with stakeholders *after* verifying the process map with the process workers and incorporating any changes to the process map so that you share an accurate, up-to-date version. You should personally conduct stakeholder meetings.

Exercise 5-2

Use Figure 5-2 to identify the stakeholders, the department they represent, when the meeting will occur, and the stakeholder's points of interest. Make certain to emphasize the appropriate point(s) of interest in the meetings.

Stakeholder Validation

Stakeholder	Department	Point(s) of Interest	Timeframe

Figure 5-2 Stakeholder Validation

2. Summary

After validating the process map and time estimates, make the appropriate changes to clarify any points of confusion on both the process map and the calculations performed in step 4 (refer to page 40, *calculating labor cost*).

Once you complete this step, you can move to step 6, improving the process, and feel comfortable that any improvement targets you set have the appropriate support from the sponsor, process workers, and stakeholders.

CHAPTER 6

Step 6:

Apply Improvement Techniques

OVERVIEW

At this point you can begin the improvement work because you have gained knowledge about:

- what the customers want from the business process (step 2)
- the existing process (step 3)
- the process and cycle time of the business process (step 4)
- the cost of the process (step 4)
- the accuracy of the process map (step 5)

Using the *customer need* and the *measurements of success* information from the scope definition document, you can set a single target or multiple improvement targets for this phase of the work.

OUTCOMES

At the end of this step, you have a new, improved business process map because you:

- Analyzed the existing process map using six improvement techniques.
- Developed an impact analysis document to keep track of the changes that have to occur in support of the new business process.
- Created a new, improved process map.

1. The Improvement Technique Wheel

The *improvement technique wheel* in Figure 6-1 shows the business process at the center of the wheel, the six techniques used to improve business processes wrapped around the process and the customer/client on the outer circle as a reminder of the importance of improving the business process in the first place.

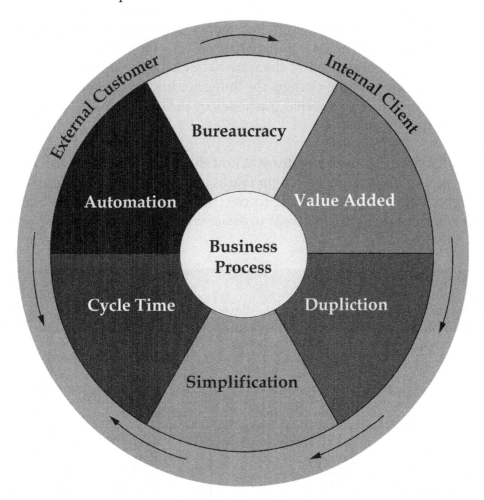

Figure 6-1 Improvement Technique Wheel

To use the improvement technique wheel, start at the top of the wheel with "bureaucracy," the first improvement technique, and move clockwise around the spokes of the wheel, ending with automation. The wheel depicts the automation technique last because you want to focus on automating an efficient, rather than an inefficient, business process. Applying the other five techniques first, ensures that you remove the process inefficiencies before moving to automation.

Focus on one technique at a time and apply it as thoroughly as possible before moving to the next technique. Go slow! Challenge the status quo. Your best tool during this step is to ask the question, "Why?"

2. Impact Analysis

The *impact analysis* outlines the changes that must happen in the organization to ensure a successful implementation of the improved business process. Create this document as you use the techniques in the improvement technique wheel.

The impact analysis example in Figure 6-2 shows how you can use the tool to capture the changes you uncover as you walk through the process map using the six improvement techniques. Each time you recognize that a change has to occur to accomplish an activity in the future state process map, make a note of the necessary change in the impact analysis, along with the rationale or reason for the change, the audience and department or business area affected by the change, and any expected pushback or problem with the proposed change in the change management column.

The change management column provides you and the project sponsor with important information to assist in proactively resolving issues prior to implementation. Collecting this information as you create the future state process (rather than after completing the process map) will help you to remember the details to assist with implementation.

REFERENCE NUMBER	PROCESS CHANGES	RATIONALE	AREA/GROUP IMPACTED	CHANGE MANAGEMENT
1	*List the change that has to occur*	*State why the change is important*	*List the audience and department(s) and/or affected group(s)*	*Identify the potential problems with the proposed change*
Example				
1	Eliminate three of the approval levels required on purchases today.	Reduces cycle time by speeding up the approval process. Gets product into retail stores quicker, thus better positioning the business in a competitive environment.	Purchasing (Senior Buyer, Purchasing Manager) Finance (Finance Manager)	Only one person in purchasing and finance will now approve buyer purchases. Because multiple levels of managers are accustomed to approving purchase orders over $10,000 today, the managers may not feel comfortable with the change.

Figure 6-2 Example of Impact Analysis

3. Improvement Targets

Before beginning the improvement step, start by identifying a few improvement targets. The targets can build off of the measurements of success you identified in step 2.

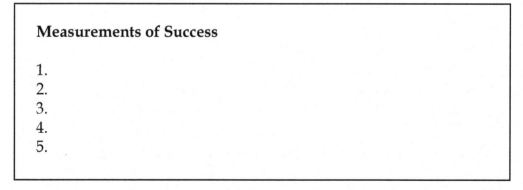

Exercise 6-1

Review the scope definition document created in step 2 and list the customer needs and measurements of success in the space provided in Figure 6-3. Based on this information, write two to five improvement targets in the space provided. Write the improvement targets as specific as possible.

Customer Needs

-
-
-
-
-

Measurements of Success

1.
2.
3.
4.
5.

Improvement Targets

1.
2.
3.
4.
5.

Figure 6-3 Improvement Targets

4. Eliminate Bureaucracy

In a business process, bureaucracy requires following a complex series of activities that hinders an effective and efficient process. The process gets bogged down in red tape, sometimes for no apparent reason. Everyone knows bureaucracy when they see it.

As you apply the improvement techniques to your business process, keep the customer needs and measurements of success in mind and consider an activity bureaucracy if it does not support one of these two items. Some questions that help to highlight bureaucratic activities include:

- How many approvals do we have in place? Why?
- How can we reduce the number of approvals required?
- Do we make decisions at the right point in the process?
- Do we generate unnecessary paperwork?
- What forms can we eliminate? If you receive push back on eliminating forms, ask, "Why do we need them?"
- How many copies of each document do we make?
- Why do we keep hardcopies?
- Do we understand what people do with the information or reports that we send them?
- Do people receive information that they do not need (or no longer require)?
- Does one person check the work of another? Why?
- How do individuals use the information requested on a form in making decisions?
- Do we have unnecessary rules?
- Does a policy or procedure get in the way?
- What will happen if an employee makes a mistake? Does the added scrutiny seem worth the expense?

SALT

You can also use the SALT filter to further help eliminate bureaucracy. **SALT** stands for:

- **S**tatutory: the activity supports legislation or a government statute
- **A**udit: examining records or transactions to check for accuracy or compliance with pre-established guidelines or rules
- **L**egal: activity supports a law, like the labor laws that control minimum wage levels and overtime pay
- **T**ax: financial charge or fee paid to a government body, like a sales tax or income tax

Exercise 6-2

Use the process map created in Figure 3-9 and highlight bureaucratic activities in blue. As you proceed through the process map, complete the impact analysis in Figure 6-4 listing activities that you plan to eliminate where you believe you may receive push back.

As you proceed through the process map, keep in mind:

- the customer needs
- measurements of success
- SALT filter
- improvement target(s)

Eliminate any activity that does not support one of these areas.

As you start applying the improvement techniques, a new process map will start to emerge. You will find blank process map templates to use in drawing the new improved process map at the end of this chapter in Figure 6-11, in chapter 12, and online at www.susanpagebooks.com.

Impact Analysis

REFERENCE NUMBER	PROCESS CHANGE(S)	RATIONALE	AREA/GROUP IMPACTED	CHANGE MANAGEMENT

Figure 6-4 Impact Analysis

Impact Analysis

REFERENCE NUMBER	PROCESS CHANGE(S)	RATIONALE	AREA/GROUP IMPACTED	CHANGE MANAGEMENT

5. Value Added

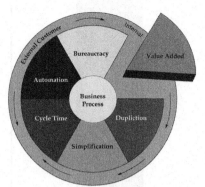

This technique requires you to examine the business process and determine if each activity contributes value to the customer. Because every step in a business process adds to the cost of the end product or service (through labor, overhead, and other expense), ask yourself if the customer would willingly pay for a step if they had knowledge of the step.

You will find that some activities you eliminate using this technique are actually bureaucratic, but you may have had a difficult time removing the activity using the first technique. The similarity between the first two techniques demonstrates the close relationship between the six improvement techniques. Once colleagues realize that an activity does not contribute value to the customer, they usually find it easier to eliminate the activity than admitting to bureaucracy.

As you move through the process map applying this technique, you will uncover activities deemed *customer* value added and *business* value added. Often, the hardest activities to eliminate are those that the business considers valuable for their own reasons because the temptation to say that an activity adds business value, instead of being a bureaucratic step, is far too easy. You have to show courage when talking about business value added activities. Remember to think strategically and keep the big picture in mind. Make the project team uncomfortable by challenging the status quo.

Exercise 6-3

Use the process map created in Figure 3-9 and highlight non-value add activities in a different color. Add activities marked for elimination, which may require further discussion, to the impact analysis in Figure 6-4 to keep track of issues you have to resolve prior to implementation.

Another alternative to color coding the process map for this technique, is to complete the value-added analysis in Figure 6-5. In this figure, you see *customer* value added, *business* value added, and *non-value* added columns. Start by listing all the activities in your process map in the first two columns, and put a check mark in one of the three columns.

The main question to ask when applying the value-added technique is, "Why does the customer care about this activity?"

Value-added Analysis

ACTIVITY NUMBER	ACTIVITY	CUSTOMER VALUE ADDED	BUSINESS VALUE ADDED	NON-VALUE ADDED

Figure 6-5 Value-added Analysis

6. Eliminate Duplication

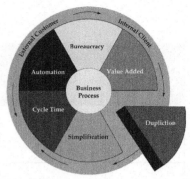

Duplication, or redundancy, occurs when multiple groups each maintain a separate set of data for their own use. Sometimes the duplication appears innocent because one group or department simply does not understand what the other group is doing; at other times, one group may not believe in the other's competence, or worse, the groups compete.

As you apply this technique, look for handoffs between departments. Handoffs often lead to duplication of effort, errors, and redundancy of information. Determine where multiple departments keep similar records, if two employees perform the same work (for example, run the same report), or perform dual data entry.

Maintaining multiple copies of a document costs labor, storage space, and can lead to legal questions surrounding "official" documentation. If you discover that no one has identified a single source of data, take the time to establish the true source of the data. This ensures *data integrity*, which means consistent, correct, and accessible data.

In evaluating duplication, look for occasions where you can:

- Establish a single source of data.
- Eliminate two employees doing the same work, like generating similar reports.
- Eliminate two people maintaining the same data.
- Eliminate the dual entry of information.
- Minimize document storage.

Exercise 6-4

Use the process map created in Figure 3-9 to highlight handoffs, areas of possible duplication, and questionable sources of data. Use the table in Figure 6-6 to capture the changes and identify the next steps.

Continue to add activities marked for elimination to the impact analysis in Figure 6-4, so that you remember to communicate with the impacted groups.

Areas of Duplication

ACTIVITY NUMBER	ACTIVITY TITLE	ISSUE	CHANGE

Figure 6-6 Areas of Duplication

7. Simplification

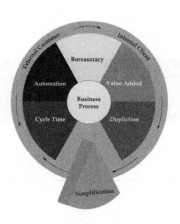

Simplification, or streamlining the process, means reducing or eliminating the complexity of a business process so that the process becomes easier to understand and more efficient. When you keep a process simple, it becomes easier to sustain and more flexible in responding to customer needs.

Simplicity relates to forms, reports, documentation, and the business process itself. Some questions that help to simplify the process include:

- What steps in the process can we streamline?
- What forms can we streamline or simplify? What unnecessary information resides on the form? Where do employees have to go to obtain the information required on the form?
- What questions do employees have when completing a form?
- How many emails are sent at any point in the process? A substantial number of emails should signal that unnecessary complexity exists.
- Where do employees go to obtain information to complete any step in the process?
- What roadblocks do we see?
- What unnecessary handoffs do we see?
- How can we standardize a step, a report, or a form to make it easier to understand?
- Do we know the number of errors made and why?
- What steps in the process can we eliminate or combine with other steps?
- Must process workers call other people to complete any step in the process? Who do they call?
- Does everyone understand the process?
- How does the organization use the data and reports throughout the process?

Exercise 6-5

Review the process map created in Figure 3-9 and identify where complexity exists. Look for how you can simplify those activities. Use Figure 6-7 to capture the changes and identify the next steps. You may uncover complex forms, reports, or documentation. You may also redesign portions of the process to reduce the number of steps required by an activity or to eliminate handoffs.

Add activities identified in this step to the impact analysis in Figure 6-4 if you expect challenges.

Simplification Opportunities

ACTIVITY NUMBER	ACTIVITY TITLE	ISSUE	CHANGE

Figure 6-7 Simplification Opportunities

8. Reduce Cycle Time

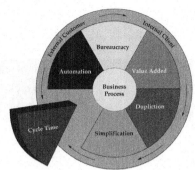

Reducing cycle time means reducing the overall time the process takes from the first activity to the last activity, including waiting or elapsed time. Customers care about cycle time because they feel it; they recognize how long it takes to receive the results. The business cares about reducing cycle time because doing so increases productivity and frees up resources.

As you work to reduce cycle time, focus on topics like:

- Why delays occur.
- Reducing handoffs.
- Reducing the waiting time that occurs between activities in the process.
- Optimizing activities that add value to the process.
- Eliminating activities that do not add value.
- Performing activities in parallel instead of one at a time.
- Combining activities.
- Benchmarking the industry standard.

Exercise 6-6

Review the process map created in Figure 3-9 and transfer the activities and cycle times to the cycle time analysis table in Figure 6-8. (Refer to the example provided in Figure 4-4 to complete the first three columns.)

After listing the activities and cycle times, highlight the activities that have the *longest* cycle times and determine how you can reduce the time for those activities.

Identify what causes the delay and list the steps to take to resolve the delay. If you identify any activities that you know will cause concern in the organization, add those items to the impact analysis in Figure 6-4, so that you have all change management-related items identified in one place.

Cycle Time Analysis

ACTIVITY NUMBER	NUMBER OF HOURS	NUMBER OF DAYS	CAUSE(S) OF DELAY	POSSIBLE RESOLUTION

Figure 6-8 Cycle Time Analysis

9. Automation

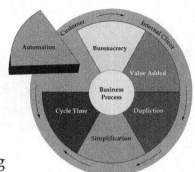

Now that you have squeezed every last bit of efficiency from the process using your analytical skills, you can look at how technology can help the process become more effective and efficient.

This technique falls last because you want to focus on automating an *efficient*, not an inefficient process. For example, you do not want to build a spreadsheet for a task that you should eliminate.

Bill Gates is credited with saying, "The first principle for any technology you contemplate introducing into a business is that automation applied to an *efficient* operation will magnify the efficiency. The second is that automation applied to an inefficient operation will just entrench the inefficiency."

In using this technique, you can focus on technology that you have available to you every day, applications that you can purchase inexpensively, or enterprise systems. Most individual employees do not have the authority to spend a few million dollars on a new computer system, so depending on your situation either focus on:

- Desktop applications available to you today (such as the Microsoft Office suite)
- Low cost applications you can purchase off the shelf (and that do not exceed your company's software approval limit for an individual purchase)
- Enterprise software applications (e.g., company-wide systems such as talent management systems)

Exercise 6-7

Identify existing technology used by your organization and list them in Figure 6-9. Include collaboration tools, intranets, and software applications (departmental and enterprise).

Next, review the process map created in Figure 3-9 and highlight activities where technology can help to automate the step. Capture this information in Figure 6-10. If you use enterprise applications, the time required to implement a solution will increase.

Update the impact analysis in Figure 6-4 with any items that may require follow up or cause concern.

Available Technology

Category	Available Technology
Desktop Technologies	
Departmental Systems	
Enterprise Applications	
Other	

Figure 6-9 Available Technology

Activities to Automate

ACTIVITY NUMBER	ACTIVITY	AUTOMATION TOOL(S)	TIME REQUIRED	RESPONSIBLE PARTY

Figure 6-10 Activities to Automate

ACTIVITY NUMBER	ACTIVITY	AUTOMATION TOOL(S)	TIME REQUIRED	RESPONSIBLE PARTY

Exercise 6-8

After applying all six improvement techniques, redraw the process map from Figure 3-9 incorporating the changes. Use Figure 6-11 to create the future state process map. You will find additional blank templates in chapter 12.

Use Figure 6-12 to complete a new detail document (replacing Figure 3-10) to support the new, improved process map. This narrative description should accompany the map because it enables employees to choose either the graphical or textual representation of the process, depending on their personal preference.

Use the impact analysis in Figure 6-4 and begin working through the organizational changes required.

Process Name _____

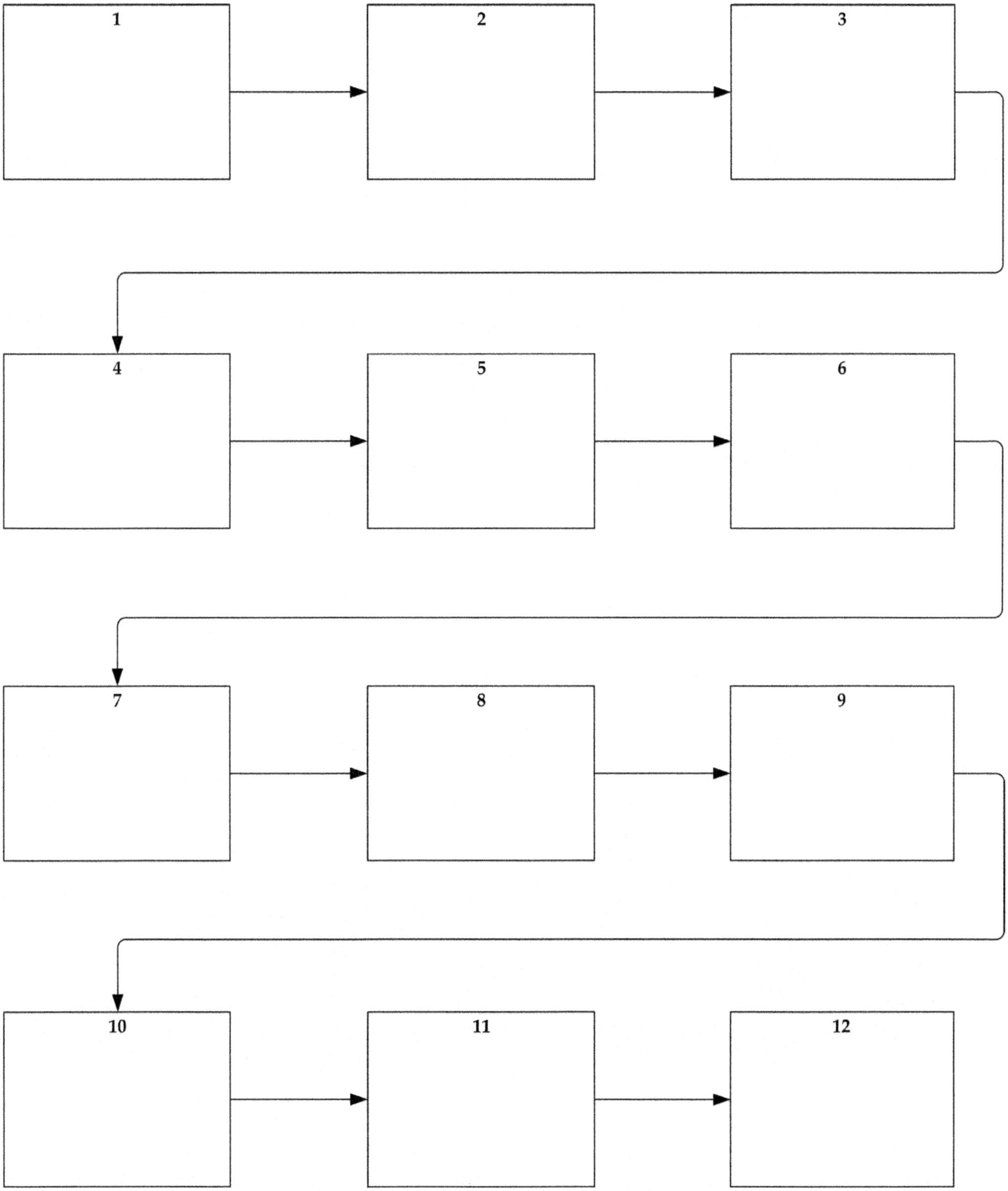

Figure 6-11 Improved Process Map

(continues)

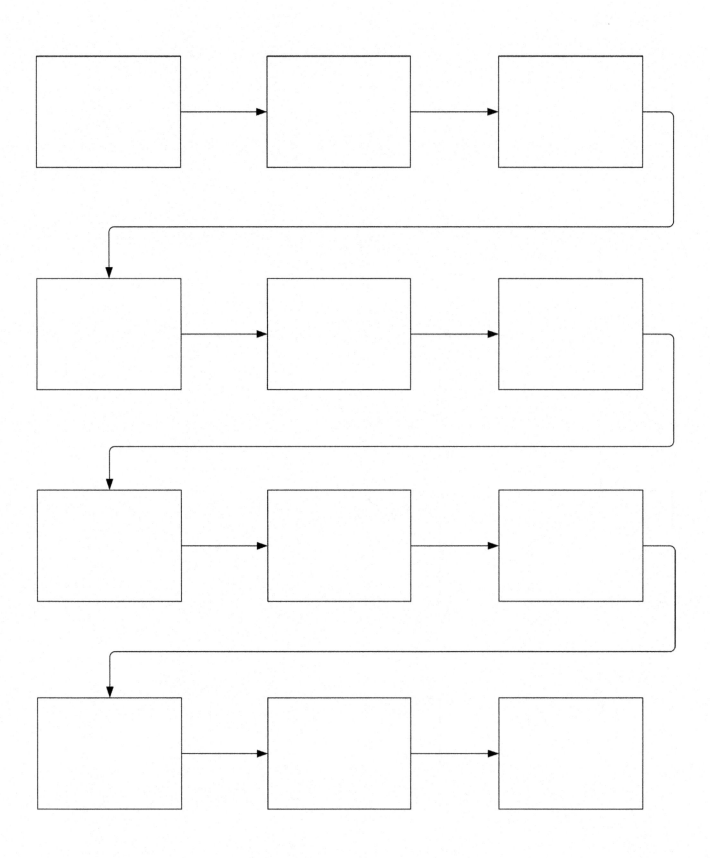

Figure 6-11 (continued)

Process Name _____

Activity Number	Activity Name and Description	Input/Output	Tools Used
1			
2			
3			
4			
5			
6			
7			
8			
9			
10			

Figure 6-12 Detail Document   *(continues)*

Activity Number	Activity Name and Description	Input/Output	Tools Used
11			
12			
13			
14			
15			

Figure 6-12 (continued)

8. Summary

Applying the six improvement techniques, one at a time, assists you in evaluating a business process in a thoughtful, planned approach. The improvement technique wheel guides you through eliminating bureaucracy, evaluating value-added activities, eliminating duplication and redundancy, simplifying the process/reports/forms, reducing cycle time, and applying automation tools.

Although the differentiation among the techniques may appear blurry at times, use the techniques one at a time because the project team will use slightly different mental filters for each technique. Applying the techniques one at a time ensures that you squeeze every last drop out of each one.

Saving the automation technique until last guarantees that you apply technology to an efficient, not an inefficient process.

At the end of this step, you have a new, improved business process that you will use for the remaining exercises in this workbook.

CHAPTER 7

Step 7:

Create Internal Controls, Tools, and Metrics

OVERVIEW

After creating the new process in Figure 6-11, the first part of this step assists you with placing internal controls on the process activities to make certain that mistakes do not occur.

The second part of this step helps you to develop details around the technology that will support the process efficiencies identified, and the third part of this step converts the *measurements of success*, defined in step 2, into metrics.

These three items bring the business process to life beyond just creating a process map and make it real for the organization.

OUTCOMES

At the end of this step, you have the following information:

- Internal controls to help prevent errors.
- Tools to help employees more easily perform their job.
- Metrics that show whether the process works as planned.

1. Internal Controls

Internal controls ensure accuracy and reliability at crucial points in a business process and help to reduce the number of errors introduced in the process. To establish internal controls, identify the points in the business process where something can go wrong.

As you work through this step, do not discuss *how* you can avoid the error until you have identified all the possible problem spots. List the problem spots first, then work on how to avoid the possible errors.

Exercise 7-1

Using the improved process map in Figure 6-11, walk through the process map activity by activity, identifying what can go wrong with each step. If a mistake can happen, signify this likelihood with a caution symbol, as shown in Figure 7-1, to denote that an error might occur and the requirement for an internal control.

Figure 7-1 Caution Symbol

As you walk through the process map, ask the question, "What can go wrong at this point?" If an activity includes the use of spreadsheets or other tools, delve into those items and again ask what problems can occur. Think of what can go wrong with everyday tools, like formulas in spreadsheets, and look for ways to avoid the errors.

After walking through the entire process map and adding caution symbols, go back to the beginning of the process map and discuss how to avoid each problem area identified. Collect this information in the internal controls document in Figure 7-2.

Example:

ACTIVITY NUMBER	ACTIVITY DESCRIPTION	POSSIBLE ISSUE(S)	INTERNAL CONTROL(S)
1	Complete recognition bonus award form	Managers across the company may not use the same criteria in justifying a recognition award or in the amount of money given to an employee.	Managers will use the justification criteria and award guidelines outlined in the *recognition award job aid* created by the compensation department. Exceptions require approval by a vice president.

Internal Controls

Activity Number	Activity Description	Possible Issue(s)	Internal Control(s)

Figure 7-2 Internal Controls

ACTIVITY NUMBER	ACTIVITY DESCRIPTION	POSSIBLE ISSUE(S)	INTERNAL CONTROL(S)

2. Tools

In step 6 you learned about the existing technology used by your company, and you took advantage of those tools to improve the business process. Now is the time to develop those tools, whether you create a spreadsheet, build a database, create job aids to help employees follow the business process, or make a change to an existing system.

If you plan to create a spreadsheet, this will go fairly fast; if you build a Microsoft Access database, this will take longer; and if you plan to make a change to your system of record (or other enterprise application), this will take even longer. At this step, you want to plan the work so that the process workers have the technology solutions available to them when you implement the change.

Exercise 7-2

Using the improved process map from Figure 6-11 and the internal controls document from Figure 7-2, list the tools requiring development in Figure 7-3. You may find some tools as simple as developing a job aid, such as a checklist, that includes the internal control activities.

In Figure 7-3, include the information required to allow you to plan the tool development:

- **Tool**: Identify the type of tool you plan to develop (spreadsheet, database, enterprise system change, job aid).
- **Development time**: Estimate how long it will take to develop each tool (e.g., thirty days); in some cases, you will have to align your development efforts with major or minor system release schedules for enterprise applications.
- **Start/End dates**: List the timeframe when tool development will occur (e.g., 4/15 through 5/10). This section helps you to align resources with the list of tools requiring development.
- **Person Responsible**: Identify the responsible resource who will develop the tool.

Tool Development Schedule

ACTIVITY NUMBER	ACTIVITY DESCRIPTION	TOOL	DEVELOPMENT TIME	START DATE	END DATE	PERSON RESPONSIBLE

(continues)

Figure 7-3 Tool Development Schedule

ACTIVITY NUMBER	ACTIVITY DESCRIPTION	TOOL	DEVELOPMENT TIME	START DATE	END DATE	PERSON RESPONSIBLE

Figure 7-3 (continued)

3. Metrics

Metrics help organizations know if the business meets performance expectations. For example, what level of customer satisfaction did the organization achieve over the past year? Metrics turn the measurements of success into specific statements that the business can report on and they allow the business to observe trends.

If you spent sufficient time thinking about the customer's needs when you established the foundation in step 2, the scope definition document helps you to define the business process metrics. Revisit Figure 6-3 and review the measurements of success and the improvement targets, thinking about them from three perspectives: effectiveness, efficiency, and adaptability.

- **Effectiveness** denotes the *quality* of the process. Does the process produce the desired results and meet the customer needs?
- **Efficiency** signifies the *productivity* of the process. Does the process minimize the use of resources and eliminate bureaucracy?
- **Adaptability** denotes the *flexibility* of the process. Does the process remain flexible in the face of changing needs?

You may find that the measurements of success are heavily weighted in favor of *effectiveness* because you wrote them from the customer's perspective and the customer is the right place to start. Because of this, you may have to think more about metrics that address efficiency and adaptability. If the measurements of success do not include efficiency or adaptability items, consider adding additional measurements of success. While you most likely cannot measure everything to begin, you should select at least one measurement of success that addresses effectiveness, efficiency, and adaptability.

When creating metrics, think about the proposed metrics and balance their usefulness with the expense of capturing the data required. Strike a balance between the value of a metric and its cost. Some people say, "If you can't measure it, you can't manage it." Albert Einstein says the opposite:

"Everything that can be counted does not necessarily count; everything that counts cannot necessarily be counted."

Exercise 7-3

Review the *measurements of success* identified in the scope definition document created in step 2 and any changes in Figure 6-3. Clarify the terminology for each measurement of success before defining a metric. For example, if you see words such as *reliable*, *quality*, or *on-demand*, spend time clarifying what these words mean.

Use Figure 7-4 to list the measurements of success and the associated metrics for your business process. Decide on the baseline to use, so that you can determine success, and identify the source of the information.

Example:

MEASUREMENT OF SUCCESS	METRIC	BASELINE	SOURCE
Increased number of new customers	30% increase in the number of "qualified" * new customers over the next six months.	Three new customers a month.	Monthly sales report

* In discussing the measurement of success in this example, the requirement surfaced to add the word "qualified" because the sales directors did not just care about volume, they also care about the quality of the new customer. The sales department has guidelines around what determines a qualified customer and part of their plan is to review the guidelines with the sales force when they introduce the new metric.

Using this example, it shows that the company currently obtains three new customers a month (the baseline), and they want to increase this number by 30% or one new customer.

Metrics

MEASUREMENT OF SUCCESS	METRIC	BASELINE	SOURCE

Figure 7-4 Metrics   *(continues)*

MEASUREMENT OF SUCCESS	METRIC	BASELINE	SOURCE

Figure 7-4 (continued)

4. Summary

Identifying points in the business process where a mistake can occur provides the opportunity to introduce internal controls. Developing an internal control document, which contains the details about how to avoid common errors, provides an effective training tool for new employees.

Developing tools to support the business process helps to improve the process. Creating job aids to simplify or standardize a step in the process, assists in training new employees and helps them to avoid errors. Planning tool development helps to determine a realistic implementation date.

Creating metrics to support the measurements of success defined in the scope definition document allows the project team to evaluate whether the process works as planned. Always show caution in developing metrics because the business can easily create too many of them. Balance the usefulness of having a metric against the expense of capturing the data required to supply the information.

CHAPTER 8

Step 8:

Test and Rework

OVERVIEW

Now that you have designed the new process, gained agreement on the changes identified in the impact analysis, and developed the tools to support the business process, you can begin to test the process to make certain that it works as expected before introducing the change to the organization.

In this step, you create a plan to test the new business process. You answer questions like whom to involve in the testing, what items to test, where to conduct the testing, when to conduct the testing, and how to conduct the testing.

OUTCOMES

At the end of this step, you should feel comfortable that the business process and tools work as planned because you have the following:

- A test plan to guide you through validating that all items work as planned.
- Time to make adjustments to the process or tools as required.
- A level of comfort that the business process will work as expected.

1. Five Steps in Testing the Business Process

Figure 8-1 provides a graphical representation of the five steps involved in testing the business process:

1. Create the test plan.
2. Develop the scenarios.
3. Implement the test plan.
4. Summarize the feedback received and rework the process and tools.
5. Retest (if appropriate).

Figure 8-1 The Five Steps in Testing a Business Process

2. Schedule

Before creating the test plan, develop a project plan for testing if not already done. Figure 8-2 provides a simple example of a testing project plan.

ID NUMBER	TASK	PERSON RESPONSIBLE	DUE DATE
1	Create the test plan (test items, goals, and objectives).	Project Manager	June 1
2	Identity testing logistics (resources, test labs, timeframe, software). Gain management support.	Project Manager	June 15
3	Conduct testing kickoff meeting (to explain process and tools).	Project Manager	July 15
4	Conduct testing.	All	July 18 - August 20
5	Rework.	Varies by issue.	ongoing through testing, ending August 30

Figure 8-2 Example of Testing Schedule

Exercise 8-1

Use Figure 8-3 to create a high-level project plan for testing.

Testing Schedule

ID Number	Task	Person Responsible	Due Date
1			
2			
3			
4			
5			
6			
7			

Figure 8-3 Testing Schedule

3. Create Test Plan

Creating a plan to test the new business process helps to organize this phase of the work, making certain that you cover all the necessary logistics and that you do not experience too many surprises during implementation. Consider it your test drive.

The test plan provides structure and a systematic approach to testing the business process and helps you to avoid mistakes. A test plan brings the who, what, where, when, and how together in one location. The discipline alone of developing a test plan forces you to think about things you might otherwise overlook. Figure 8-4 outlines the components of a test plan.

ITEM NUMBER	TASK	DEFINITION
1	Define testing goal.	A statement of the overall purpose for the testing.
2	Define testing method.	Describes the procedures used to conduct the testing. It answers the who, what, where, when, and how questions. • Who will perform the tests? • What items to include in the test plan? • Where will the testing occur? • When will the testing occur? • How will you communicate with the testers? • How will you report, track, and resolve problems?
3	Define objectives for test items.	A statement that helps the project team to write appropriate test scenarios - what do you want to accomplish for each test item identified in number two?
4	Develop scenarios for test items.	Step-by-step guidelines to assist the testing resources understand how to test the process and tools, and the expected outcomes.
5	Gain support for resources.	Identify the specific resource names required and gain agreement from management. In number two you indicated the group(s) or department(s) involved; now you identify the actual employee names.
6	Create feedback collection tool.	A spreadsheet to help you track defects that occur during the testing.
7	Conduct testing.	The period of time testing will occur.
8	Rework, as required.	The time allocated to complete the rework.

Figure 8-4 Test Plan Framework

TESTING GOAL AND OBJECTIVES

The testing goal helps you to stay focused on the overall purpose for testing. The objectives in number three explain what to test on each item that you identified as part of the testing method (the second bullet in item number two).

Example

Testing Goal: To validate that the budgeting process is simple for managers to use on a global basis, and that the tools created to support the process work as expected with no defects.

Testing Objective

TEST ID	TEST ITEM	OBJECTIVE	RESOURCES	TIMEFRAME
1	Calculation Tool	Validate that the formulas work correctly in the Microsoft Excel spreadsheet, and that the user cannot change the field values.	Sarah Mei	July 18 - 22

Exercise 8-2

Using Figure 8-4 as a reference, answer item numbers 1, 2, 3, 5, and 7 in Figure 8-5 for the business process you created in Figure 6-11.

Test Plan

ITEM NUMBER	ITEM	CONTENT	
1	Testing Goal		
2	Testing Method	(a) Who to include *(include titles and department)*	
		(b) What items to test *(identify each tool or part of the process you want to test)*	▪ ▪ ▪ ▪ ▪

Figure 8-5 Test Plan

ITEM NUMBER	ITEM	CONTENT	
		(c) When to conduct testing *(decide the best time to test based on operational constraints)*	
		(d) Where to conduct testing *(determine if you have to test in various locations)*	
		(e) Communication plan *(determine how frequently and the method by which you plan to communicate with testers to discuss problems)*	
		(f) Problem resolution plan *(identify the process you plan to use to resolve problems)*	
3	Testing Objectives	Objective by test item *(refer to 2b)*	▪ ▪ ▪ ▪ ▪
4	Scenarios	Reference to location of scenarios and data sheets	
5	Resource Names	Specific tester names	
6	Feedback Tool	Develop tool	
7	Conduct Testing	Date and times	
8	Rework	Date and times	

4. Develop Scenarios

Test scenarios help to guide the testing resources, so that they know the details of what to test. In the examples that follow, the "expected result" column is critical to complete because the testing resources have to understand what *should* happen after executing a step in the scenario. The tester writes the actual outcome they experience in the "actual result" column.

You should write various alternatives for the business process as part of your test plan. You can either create a separate scenario for each alternative set of data you want to test (example 1) or create a generic scenario and use data sheets to supply the different data sets (example 2).

Example 1 (single test scenario with data included)

Test scenario: Calculation tool
Responsible tester: Finance department

Step	Description	Data	Expected Result	Actual Result
1 of 7	Open spreadsheet	None	File opens with no pop-up messages	
2 of 7	Enter data in cells A2, A3, and A4.	A2: 485 A3: 500 A4: 715	Cell A5 displays 1700	

Example 2 (generic test scenario with reference to data sheets)

Test scenario: Calculation tool
Responsible tester: Finance department

STEP	DESCRIPTION	DATA	EXPECTED RESULT	ACTUAL RESULT
1 of 7	Open spreadsheet	See data sheet 5	File opens with no pop-up messages	
2 of 7	Enter data in cells A2, A3, and A4.	See data sheet 5	Cell A5 displays: 1: 1,700 2: 2,635 3: 18,000 4: 72,527	

Data sheet 5 lists the different data values to test.

Example of Data Sheet 5

STEP	DATA SET 1	DATA SET 2	DATA SET 3	DATA SET 4
1 of 7	None	None	None	None
2 of 7	A2: 485 A3: 500 A4: 715	A2: 750 A3: 895 A4: 990	A2: 2,500 A3: 7,500 A4: 8,000	A2: 17,580 A3: 22,380 A4: 32,567

Exercise 8-3

After creating the test plan, use Figure 8-6 to develop a single test scenario or combine it with Figure 8-7 to create a supporting data sheet. The test scenarios become part of the overall test plan.

Test scenario:
Responsible tester:

STEP	DESCRIPTION	DATA	EXPECTED RESULT	ACTUAL RESULT

Figure 8-6 Test Scenario

Step	Description	Data	Expected Result	Actual Result

Test scenario:
Data sheet number:

STEP	DATA SET 1	DATA SET 2	DATA SET 3	DATA SET 4

Figure 8-7 Data Sheet

5. Feedback Tool and Rework

Use a spreadsheet to collect issues during testing, and store it in a collaborative space, so that all testers can record their findings. You can use a shared network drive or a tool such as Microsoft SharePoint to allow the entire project team access to the spreadsheet.

Include information on the spreadsheet that you want testers to provide. For example, you can include severity levels, such as *High*, *Medium*, and *Low*, to help prioritize critical errors. You can also categorize errors into different types, for example, *Usability* or *Functionality*.

Example

ID NUMBER	TEST ITEM	DATE DETECTED	DESCRIPTION OF ERROR	SEVERITY	DETECTED BY	ASSIGNED TO
1	Calculation tool	7/25	Pop-up message appears when opening the file that asks if the user wants to enable macros.	Low	Tom Wilhelm	Isaac Mussini

Review and resolve issues during the testing period. Once you complete testing, decide whether more rework has to occur and whether you have to retest a portion of the process. View testing as an iterative process where you test an item. If the item does not work, you fix it, but then you have to test it again.

Exercise 8-4

Create a spreadsheet using Figure 8-8 to collect defect information during the testing period.

Use this information during daily phone meetings to discuss the problems encountered and the status of problem resolution.

Issue Resolution Log

ID Number	Test Item	Date	Description of Error	Severity	Detected By	Assigned To

Figure 8-8 Issue Resolution Log

6. Summary

Creating a plan to test the new business process helps to make certain that it works as expected and that you have a successful implementation.

The discipline of creating a test plan forces you to answer questions such as who you should include in the testing, what items to test, where to conduct the testing, and when is the best time to conduct the testing.

Test scenarios (or scripts) provide structure for the resources performing the testing by providing them with step-by-step instructions to conduct the test. Gathering information in an issue resolution log provides you with the information to understand what has to change in the business process or with the tools.

Fix issues as they occur during testing, and once the testing is done, decide if the business process requires any major changes. Once you know that everything works as planned, you can begin implementation.

CHAPTER 9

Step 9:

Implement the Change

OVERVIEW

Now that you know the business process and tools work, plan how you will introduce the change to the organization. Who needs to know? What do they need to know? When should you inform them? How should you communicate the change?

The term *change management* simply means taking people in an organization from the current state to the future state. Change is a constant and the Greek philosopher Heraclitus wrote: "Nothing endures but change."

This step focuses on developing the implementation, training, and communication plans.

OUTCOMES

At the end of this step, you should feel prepared to introduce the new business process to the organization because you have the following:

- An implementation plan to guide you through the entire project.
- A training plan that defines the audience, learning objectives, methodology, facilitator, and dates.
- A communication plan that defines the audience, goal, key message points, vehicles, and dates.

1. Implementation Plan

The best implementation plans include *phases* that break the work down into reasonable chunks that function as a guide to keep the work on track. Figure 9-1 shows a Microsoft Project example of an implementation (or project) plan with three phases identified:

- **The design phase** identifies the work involved in defining and improving the business process.
- **The development phase** includes creating the tools required to make the improved business process work before moving to step 8, where you test the process and tools.
- **The implementation phase** includes testing the process, determining how to roll out the new business process, how to communicate and train the affected people, and how to continually improve the business process so that it remains relevant over time.

You can break a phase down further by using the concept of "tracks" that help to further organize the work. If you use a tool like Microsoft Project, you can more easily keep track of predecessors (tasks that must finish before another task can start).

Project Plan

Microsoft Project - Project Plan3

File   Edit   View   Insert   Format   Tools   Project   Collaborate   Window   Help   Adobe PDF

No Group

Tasks ▾ | Resources ▾ | Track ▾ | Report ▾

	Task Name	Duration	Start	Finish	Predecessors	Resource Names
1	⊟ DESIGN PHASE	26 days	Thu 4/1/10	Thu 5/6/10		
2	Establish Foundation	1 day	Thu 4/1/10	Thu 4/1/10		Project Team
3	Map Business Process	5 days	Fri 4/2/10	Thu 4/8/10	2	Project Team
4	Estimate Time and Cost	3 days	Fri 4/9/10	Tue 4/13/10	3	Project Team
5	Verify Process Map	5 days	Fri 4/9/10	Thu 4/15/10	3	Project Team
6	Apply Improvement Techniques	10 days	Fri 4/16/10	Thu 4/29/10	5	Project Team
7	Create Internal Controls/metrics	5 days	Fri 4/30/10	Thu 5/6/10	6	Project Team
8						
9	⊟ DEVELOPMENT PHASE	30 days	Fri 4/30/10	Thu 6/10/10		
10	Develop Tool 1 - Reference Card	15 days	Fri 4/30/10	Thu 5/20/10	6	Jim Stein
11	Develop Tool 2 - Access Database	20 days	Fri 4/30/10	Thu 5/27/10	6	Francois Bling
12	Develop Report Specifications	5 days	Fri 4/30/10	Thu 5/6/10	6	Wendy Chan
13	Gain Client Approval of Report Specifications	0.67 days	Fri 5/7/10	Fri 5/7/10	12	Wendy Chan,Sponsor
14	Develop Report	10 days	Fri 5/28/10	Thu 6/10/10	13,11,12	Wendy Chan
15						
16	⊟ IMPLEMENTATION PHASE	72 days	Fri 5/7/10	Mon 8/16/10		
17	⊟ Testing Track	23 days	Fri 6/11/10	Tue 7/13/10		.
18	⊞ Develop Test Plan	8 days	Fri 6/11/10	Tue 6/22/10		
25	Implement Test Plan	10 days	Wed 6/23/10	Tue 7/6/10	18	Project Team
26	Rework, as necessary	5 days	Wed 7/7/10	Tue 7/13/10	25	Project Team
27	⊟ Communication Track	13 days	Wed 7/14/10	Fri 7/30/10		
28	⊞ Develop Communication Plan	8 days	Wed 7/14/10	Fri 7/23/10		
34	⊞ Develop Communication Vehicles	5 days	Mon 7/26/10	Fri 7/30/10		
44	⊟ Training Track	18 days	Wed 7/14/10	Fri 8/6/10		
45	⊞ Develop Training Plan	3 days	Wed 7/14/10	Fri 7/16/10		
51	Develop/Customize Training Materials	10 days	Mon 7/19/10	Fri 7/30/10	45	Jim Stein
52	Schedule Training	0.5 days	Mon 7/19/10	Mon 7/19/10	45	Jim Stein
53	Conduct Training	5 days	Mon 8/2/10	Fri 8/6/10	52,51	Project Team
54	⊟ Change Management Track	72 days	Fri 5/7/10	Mon 8/16/10		
55	Develop Impact Analysis	5 days	Fri 5/7/10	Thu 5/13/10	1	Project Manager
56	Identify Responsible Person to Address Changes	0.5 days	Fri 5/14/10	Fri 5/14/10	55	Project Manager
57	Id Strategy	days	Mon 8/9/10			Project Ma

Figure 9-1 Example of Project Plan

Exercise 9-1

Use Figure 9-2 to develop an implementation plan for your business process improvement project and include the concept of phases and tracks. If you have project management software, feel free to use that instead of the figure provided.

Implementation Plan

Task ID	Task Name	Duration	Start	Finish	Predecessors	Resource

(continues)

Figure 9-2 Implementation Plan

Implementation Plan

TASK ID	TASK NAME	DURATION	START	FINISH	PREDECESSORS	RESOURCE

Figure 9-2 (continued)

2. Training Plan

In developing the training plan, identify what training has to occur to make sure that all parties understand and can perform their process responsibilities. Think about:

- Who requires the training?
- Who owns the responsibility to conduct the training?
- What topics do the participants have to know?
- Where should you conduct the training?
- When should you train?
- What methods will you use to conduct the training?

Although some people use the terms *training* and *communication* interchangeably, they are two different streams of work, and anyone in the training field probably has experience with a client trying to make a communication problem a training problem.

Definitions:

- **Communication** transmits or exchanges information and messages.
- **Training** provides a person with the knowledge and skills to perform a task.

As you write learning objectives for the training, start each one with an action verb that denotes the ability to do something (e.g., run, identify, explain, complete). What should a person be able to *do* after completing training? In business process work, you generally want a person to either:

- *Apply* something (highest level of cognition).
- *Absorb* or grasp something (middle level of cognition).
- *Know* something (lowest level of cognition).

The *know-absorb-apply* example demonstrates a hierarchy that exists where the participant attending training achieves a higher level of competence as they move up the hierarchy. Figure 9-3 shows a visual representation of the hierarchy of learning. In this figure, first you *know*, then you *absorb*, and finally you *apply*.

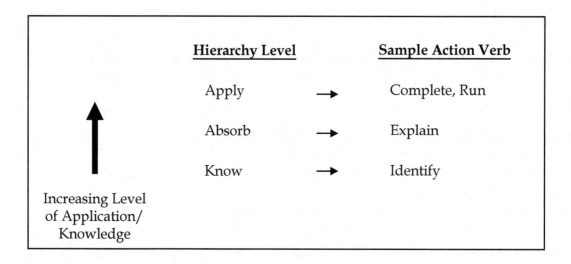

Figure 9-3 Hierarchy of Learning Objectives

Exercise 9-2

Create a training plan for your new business process using Figure 9-4. List the different categories of people that you have to train in the audience column. Write learning objectives for each audience, indicate how you will train them (methodology), list the tools you plan to create, identify who will deliver the training (facilitator), and include the time of the training (due date).

Example

AUDIENCE	LEARNING OBJECTIVE	METHODOLOGY	TOOLS	FACILITATOR	DUE DATE
Manager	*Run* the new report.	Meeting	Reference card	Analyst	October 15

Training Plan

AUDIENCE	LEARNING OBJECTIVE	METHODOLOGY	TOOLS	FACILITATOR	DUE DATE

Figure 9-4 Training Plan

3. Communication Plan

In developing the communication plan, think about what messaging has to occur to make sure that all parties receive the appropriate information to prepare them for the change. Introducing a new business process is like introducing any other change to an organization. After defining the audience (the who), determine the following for each audience group:

- **Goal** (the why): Identify the purpose for the communication.
- **Key message points** (the what): Explain what each audience group has to know about the change.
- **Communication vehicles** to use (the how): The best method to use in communicating with an audience.
- **Due date** for the communication (the when): The right time to communicate with an audience.

Exercise 9-3

Create a communication plan for your new business process using Figure 9-5. List the different categories of people that you have to communicate with in the audience column. Write the communication goal and key message points for each audience. Decide how you will communicate with each audience (method), and the timing of the communication (due date).

Example

Audience	Communication Goal	Key Message Points	Communication Vehicles (Method)	Due Date
Customer	Feedback and support	• What's changing linked to the customer needs defined in the scope definition document • Benefits to the customer • Timeline	Phone call; written follow-up	October 15
Process Workers	Education	• What's changing and why • Their role and responsibility • Training schedule • Contact resources for help	Meeting (live and via video conference); intranet site	October 18

Communication Plan

AUDIENCE	COMMUNICATION GOAL	KEY MESSAGE POINTS	COMMUNICATION VEHICLES (METHOD)	DUE DATE

Figure 9-5 Communication Plan

4. Summary

Planning the entire business process improvement project up front, by creating the implementation plan, will give you confidence that you have the right steps and the right people in place to accomplish the work. The implementation plan is the framework that brings the separate components together including:

- **The project plan** that organizes the entire work effort.
- **The training plan** that tells who needs training on what.
- **The communication plan** that identifies who needs to know what about the new business process.

Note

The project team (or manager) can decide when to develop the implementation or project plan. Project plans are typically developed before the start of a project, while an implementation plan can occur later and focus on just the changes that have to occur to introduce the new process to the organization.

CHAPTER 10

Step 10:
Drive Continuous Improvement

OVERVIEW

DEFINITION: Continuous improvement, a term derived from the total quality movement, means monitoring a business process and making adjustments to it, so that it continues to improve over time.

Developing a continuous improvement *plan* and *schedule* translates a vague concept such as "continuous improvement" into a tool to make certain that the process continues to deliver the gains achieved. This means continually measuring the business process, regularly evaluating customer needs and expectations, engaging the process workers on a regular basis, and not allowing the documentation to sit on the shelf and collect dust.

Continuous improvement requires a change in mindset, where you accept that improvement never ends and that you may never achieve perfection. As you follow the ten steps to business process improvement, you acquire a unique level of understanding about the business process, which positions you to act in the role of innovator, influencer, and communicator. You can then:

- Demonstrate innovation by continually identifying new ways to improve the business process.
- Influence others to continuously think about their work from a process perspective.
- Continue to talk and communicate with customers, stakeholders, and process workers to validate that the process continues to deliver what they require.

OUTCOMES

At the end of this step, you have the following:

- Details about how to adapt the business process to changing business needs.
- A plan that includes the appropriate steps to regularly review the business process.
- A schedule that provides a snapshot of when to evaluate multiple business processes so that you can manage a group of business processes.

1. The Continuous Improvement Cycle

The continuous improvement cycle in Figure 10-1 shows four phases that will help you with this step. Each phase in the cycle provides a degree of structure to help you think about continually improving a business process. You can move through the four phases quickly, but do so often. The four phases include:

1. **Evaluate**: Determine the opportunities.
2. **Test**: Make the change and try it out on a limited basis.
3. **Assess**: Determine whether the change worked.
4. **Execute**: Deploy the change on a wide scale.

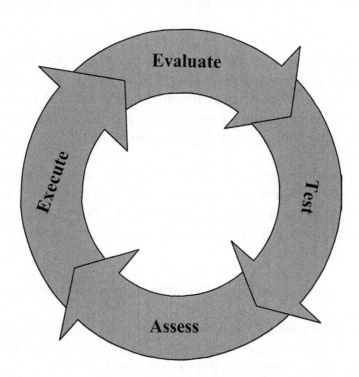

Figure 10-1 Continuous Improvement Cycle

Evaluate

In this phase of continuous improvement, examine all aspects of the business process to identify opportunities for improvement. To accomplish this you have to understand the expectations for the business process. Start by asking a few questions: Does the process continue to deliver the effectiveness, efficiency, and adaptability intended? What bottlenecks exist? Have customer needs changed?

You should spend the majority of your time in the evaluate phase of the continuous improvement cycle. How frequently you revisit this phase depends on how often the business uses the process. If it is an ongoing process, used daily, go through this phase more frequently, but if it is a cyclical process, used annually or semiannually, go through this phase less often.

During this phase, look at the process itself and confirm that everyone follows the process, uses the tools as planned, and gathers the metrics as defined. This includes items like:

- Talking to the customers and stakeholders to assess how they feel about the effectiveness of the process. This provides qualitative feedback instead of numbers, and both qualitative and quantitative data assist in determining the effectiveness of the process.
- Determining the effectiveness of the internal controls put in place. Do they help in eliminating errors?
- Evaluating the roles and responsibilities and making changes if appropriate.
- Making sure that the organization trains new employees.
- Evaluating the effectiveness of any communication processes.
- Making certain that employees share information and knowledge.
- Making sure that vendors or suppliers deliver what the process expects.

Test

Once you have identified a problem or opportunity, made the process changes, and established an improvement goal, implement the change on a small scale to validate that the change(s) work. In this phase of continuous improvement, you want to make certain that any changes work before introducing them on a wide scale.

This task should seem familiar since step 8 covered testing in detail. You can use many of the same techniques from that step here, just on a smaller scale. Remember to think about the who, what, where, when, and how of testing the change:

- **Who** to involve in the test
- **What** items to test
- **Where** the test should occur
- **When** the test should occur
- **How** to measure the success of the change

Identify who will participate, what part of the business process to test, what location or area to include in the test, how long the test will run, how to collect test data, and how to define success. Include the process owner, or sponsor, to make certain that you have the appropriate support.

Depending on what you uncover in the evaluate phase of the continuous improvement cycle, you may not always have to test because in some cases employees simply require training or the business may simply have to make adjustments to the measurement data. At other times though, if you make significant changes you have to test those changes before implementing them on a wide scale. If you find yourself making major changes, revisit step 8 and create a test plan.

Assess

In this phase of continuous improvement, keep track of how the changes work as you implement the change on a small scale, to understand what has to occur to introduce the change on a wider scale. Did the change deliver the value expected? What other criteria should you consider?

In this phase, review the data collected during the testing phase, make any adjustments deemed appropriate, and decide whether to proceed with the changes. You may also want to bring in benchmark data to help you form an opinion on what changes to introduce.

Execute

After assessing the success of the changes to the business process and perhaps comparing the process to other internal groups or external companies, you can deploy the updated business process across the organization.

This phase should seem similar to the implementation step discussed in step 9, but on a smaller scale. In this phase, train the process workers on the change and communicate the change to affected parties. Although you do not have to recreate a training plan or a communication plan, you should create a new impact analysis.

The same audience defined in the original training and communication plans have to know about the process changes if the changes affect them. The training plan will have a reduced number of learning objectives and perhaps a different, simpler approach; and the communication plan can probably use the same goal, key message points, and communication vehicles defined in the plan.

2. Continuous Improvement Plan

The continuous improvement *plan* summarizes the activities necessary to maintain a focus on the business process and outlines how frequently to perform each activity, the sources of data required, the technique or method to use, and who will perform the activity.

Figure 10-2 shows an example of a plan you can use as a starting point for your business process, and you will discover that the activities remain fairly consistent for any business process. This example shows a training and development process.

ACTIVITY	FREQUENCY	DATA SOURCE	METHOD	PERSON RESPONSIBLE
Review measurement date	Monthly	Weekly activity reports	Staff meeting; conversation	Training manager
Revisit customer needs	Semiannual	Scope definition document (SDD)	SDD review; survey; follow up phone call	Director, training and development
Test internal controls	Monthly	Process map and internal control checklist	Internal control document review; observation; conversation	Training manager
Validate process workers follow the process	Quarterly	Process map and detail document	Process map review; observation; conversation	Training manager
Revisit stakeholder needs	Semiannual	Scope definition document	Email; follow up phone call	Director, training and development
Evaluate third-party performance	Annual	Process map and detail document	Process map review; phone call	Training manager

Figure 10-2 Example of Continuous Improvement Plan

- **Review measurement data**: Look at what the project team identified as measurements of success in step 2 and how you decided to measure those items in step 7.
- **Revisit customer needs**: Revisit customer expectations identified in step 2.
- **Test internal controls**: Review the new process map resulting from step 6, looking for the internal control icon and reviewing how the project team stated the business would overcome the potential problems in the internal control checklist.
- **Validate process workers follow process**: Walk through the process map and validate that the employees involved in the process follow the steps outlined.

- **Revisit stakeholder needs**: Revisit the stakeholder expectations identified in step 2.
- **Evaluate third-party performance**: Review the process map and validate that the vendors or suppliers are delivering what the process specifies.

Exercise 10-1

Review the scope definition document created in step 2, the new process map resulting from step 6, the metrics identified in step 7, and think about the customer, process workers, stakeholders, and vendors/suppliers you identified. Using Figure 10-3 decide how frequently you plan to review each of the activities listed in the figure, what data source you will use, how you plan to perform the activity, and who has responsibility for the activity. If you want to use different activities, use the blank matrix in Figure 10-4 to create a continuous improvement plan.

ACTIVITY	FREQUENCY	DATA SOURCE	METHOD	PERSON RESPONSIBLE
Review measurement date				
Revisit customer needs				
Test internal controls				
Validate process workers follow the process				
Revisit stakeholder needs				
Evaluate third-party performance				

Figure 10-3 Continuous Improvement Plan

Continuous Improvement Plan

ACTIVITY	FREQUENCY	DATA SOURCE	METHOD	PERSON RESPONSIBLE

Figure 10-4 Continuous Improvement Plan

3. Continuous Improvement Schedule

As the inventory of improved business processes increases, create one continuous improvement *schedule* that includes all the business processes to keep track of the various activity. Translate the frequencies, from Figure 10-3 or 10-4, to actual dates, so that the business has an annual schedule to follow.

Figure 10-5 shows an example for part of a recruitment department's hiring processes with the standard activities from Figure 10-3 listed horizontally as column headers. This allows you to list the business processes vertically down the left-hand column, which provides a summary of all business processes in one document. Notice how the figure lists three of the recruitment department's processes (requisition, sourcing, and orientation) down the left-hand column.

BUSINESS PROCESS	REVIEW MEASUREMENT DATA	TEST INTERNAL CONTROLS	REVISIT CUSTOMER NEEDS	VALIDATE PROCESS WORKERS	REVISIT STAKEHOLDER NEEDS	EVALUATE THIRD PARTIES
Requisition	1st of month	January July	April	January July	April	December
Sourcing	15th of month	March September	June	March September	June	December
Orientation	30th of month	May	August	November	August	December

Figure 10-5 Example of Continuous Improvement Schedule

Figure 10-5 shows that the business wants to review the measurement data the most frequently (monthly) and plans to look at the metrics for the requisition process on the first of each month, sourcing on the fifteenth, and orientation on the thirtieth. This figure also shows that the business will review the customer, stakeholder, and third party data least frequently (annually).

Exercise 10-2

Create a continuous improvement schedule for the business process you just improved using Figure 10-6. As you finish improving additional business processes, continue to add them to the schedule.

You can see how much easier it gets to manage multiple business processes by having a snapshot because you can quickly see what the business has to focus on at any point in time.

Continuous Improvement Schedule

BUSINESS PROCESS	REVIEW MEASUREMENT DATA	TEST INTERNAL CONTROLS	REVISIT CUSTOMER NEEDS	VALIDATE PROCESS WORKERS	REVISIT STAKEHOLDER NEEDS	EVALUATE THIRD PARTIES

Figure 10-6 Continuous Improvement Schedule

4. Summary

The continuous improvement cycle confirms that the business process continually delivers effectiveness, efficiency, and adaptability to the organization. The four phases (evaluate, test, assess, and execute) provide the necessary structure. You can move through the four phases quickly, but do so often. Let the frequency of how often the business uses a business process drive the continuous improvement plan and schedule. During continuous improvement, spend the majority of your time in the evaluate phase because improvement opportunities surface in this phase.

Throughout continuous improvement, you will find yourself using some of the tools created during previous steps, like the scope definition document from step 2, the impact analysis from step 6, or the training and communication plans from step 9. Continually evaluate the information defined in the scope definition document because it helps to keep the business process aligned with the changing business needs.

The continuous improvement *plan* lays the foundation for verifying that the business process remains relevant and adapts to changing business needs. Combining all your business processes into one continuous improvement *schedule* provides a tool to better manage the work throughout the year.

CHAPTER 11

Create the Executive Summary

OVERVIEW

This chapter shows how to organize the business process work into an executive summary, a package that management will find useful.

Executive summaries differ and no two ever look exactly alike because each situation has its own unique circumstances. Executive summaries usually range from one to ten pages, but there is no standard, so feel free to create what seems right for your particular situation.

The most important point when writing an executive summary is to make certain that it addresses what the sponsor (or other executive audiences) cares about, so tailor the summary to address those known concerns.

In business process work, the executive summary provides a high-level overview of the entire project. Write the summary in a clear and concise manner, and provide additional details in an appendix, if needed. When writing the executive summary, remember that not every reader has the same degree of familiarity with the topic as you, so write with the novice reader in mind.

OUTCOMES

At the end of this step, you have the following:

- The framework to summarize your work
- The knowledge of how to write an executive summary

1. The Six Sections of the Executive Summary

Start the executive summary with an intriguing or compelling statement that grabs the reader's attention, and include the following sections:

- Project focus
- Goals
- Summary
- Key findings
- Deliverables
- Appendix (if applicable)

PROJECT FOCUS

Start the executive summary with a story about the current condition that illustrates the problems that caused you to take on the work. I use project focus instead of problem statement, because the word *focus* is more positive than *problem*, putting the reader in a more positive mindset. Include information in the project focus that shows the business need that drove the analysis; for example, did the work result from a reorganization, the formation of a new business, an increase in errors, or another reason?

The intent of the opening paragraphs is to enable the reader to instantly understand why the project team focused on the specific business process. Provide enough detail so that you paint the picture of the current situation from the reader's perspective rather than from your own.

GOALS

The project goals become the second part of the executive summary. Think of a goal as an objective or the purpose of your work. When listing the goals of the project, revisit the scope definition document you created and review what the customer and stakeholders told you they wanted from the process. Then look at the measurements of success that you defined. This information assists you in articulating the goals to include in this section. Simply state the goals in bullet fashion and keep them short.

SUMMARY

The summary should tell the story of your journey. You can think of this third section of the executive summary as an executive summary within the executive summary. Executives generally spend their time reading the project focus and the summary sections, skimming over goals and deliverables. As a result, devote sufficient time to this section.

If your work included a cross-functional group of employees, identify the project team membership to show the integration between departments, a point that management will appreciate. Link what you write in this section to the goals identified in the prior section, and include various analytical results to give the reader a few concrete statistics to identify with, such as a labor summary or information from the impact analysis or implementation.

KEY FINDINGS

The purpose of this section of the executive summary is to make management aware of the key points uncovered during the work. The topics may relate to what the project team learned or to cautions about crucial points in the process. Focus on the few points important for the reader to remember.

DELIVERABLES

In this section, identify the materials created as a result of the business process work. List the title and description of each deliverable. The recap helps readers understand what information to ask for if they want additional details. Deliverables can include documents such as:

- Process overview
- Process map
- Detail document
- Internal controls document
- Checklists
- Impact analysis
- Implementation plan
- Training plan
- Communication plan

APPENDIX

Include any additional content in the appendix. If you want to include numerous pieces of information, break the appendix down into separate ones and number them. The appendix may include feedback you received from the project team, how the team completed the work, a customized version of the roadmap, the scope definition document, process definitions if you addressed multiple business processes, and perhaps the process map(s). Include whatever material you feel supports your conclusions.

Exercise 11-1

Create an Executive Summary using the template in Figure 11-1, and identify one to two summaries you plan to include.

Executive Summary
<Name of Business Process>

PROJECT FOCUS

GOALS
The goals of the process work are to ensure that the business process: ■ ■ ■ ■ ■

Figure 11-1 Executive Summary

SUMMARY

KEY FINDINGS

DELIVERABLES

2. Summary

Creating an executive summary gives you the opportunity to summarize your work for management and gain recognition, while appearing like a normal part of any project closure.

Keep the readers in mind when writing the executive summary, and include the information you know they care about reading. The project focus sets the tone for the entire executive summary and either draws readers in or bores them. Include the goals of the work, a summary of the work itself, the key findings, and a list of the deliverables.

Include process data in the summary section of the executive summary to show the analytical nature of your work because managers always care about the efficient use of head count and the delivery of effective processes to the customers. Keep effectiveness, efficiency, and adaptability in your thoughts as you write the executive summary.

CHAPTER 12

Tools and Templates

OVERVIEW

This chapter provides tools and copies of templates used throughout the workbook. Use the information as a quick reference guide when facilitating business process improvement work.

You can use the space provided in the previous chapters to answer the questions in the *question guide* or use the space provided in this chapter. This chapter also covers building consensus and ideas for how to practice using the material.

OUTCOMES

At the end of this chapter, you have the following:

- A handy question guide that you can use throughout your process improvement work.
- A better understanding of how following the ten steps leads to building consensus.
- An idea for how to practice the material before using it in your business.

Question Guide

The question guide provides sample questions to ask during each of the ten steps to business process improvement (BPI). As you use the question guide, remember three important points:

1. **Hesitate** after you ask a question, especially the first question. Do not rush. It should feel a little uncomfortable for you as a facilitator and for the project team, but wait until the project team answers. If you answer the first question, you will find yourself responsible for answering most questions.

2. Ask **why** frequently because it will prove to be one of your best weapons in completing BPI work. Even when the project team gives you an answer, you can ask why as a follow-up question to further fine-tune the process.

3. Use **open-ended** questions instead of closed questions. Ask **what/how** instead of "can." Instead of asking, "Can we....." change the question to, "What....." For example, instead of asking, "Can we combine any activities?" ask, "What activities can we combine?" "How can we combine activities?" Avoid asking questions that have a yes or no answer.

Step 1: Prioritizing Business Processes

Question	Answer
☐ What criteria should we consider in prioritizing our business processes?	
☐ What main categories should we use? » How should we define each category? » Discuss each category you decide to use and further explain what it means. For example, what does *impact* mean? Using the four recommended categories as a starting point, you may ask: • *Impact*: How much does the business process affect the business? • *Implementation*: How feasible is it to make changes? • *Current State*: How well is the process working today? • *Value*: What is the benefit, or return, of improving the process?	
☐ Have we included what our customers, clients, stakeholders, and third parties care about?	
☐ Is there anything else important for us to consider?	
☐ What scale should we use? You can use a 1-3 scale, a 1-10 scale, or any other scale that makes sense for the business.	
☐ Should we apply a weight to the categories? If so, what weight should we apply to each category? Assign weights so that the total of all categories equal 100.	

STEP 2: SCOPE DEFINITION DOCUMENT

QUESTION	ANSWER
☐ Process Owner: Who has ultimate responsibility for the business process? This is not necessarily your boss or the project sponsor.	
☐ Description: » How would you describe the business process to a person new or unfamiliar with it? » Is there anything specifically *out of scope*? Are there any exclusions? List those items. » Consider terminology used and ask for a definition of any unusual or technical term. You may say, "I think that I know what *candidate* means, but can you define it, so that we are all on the same page?" » Give me an example.	
☐ Scope: » Where does the business process begin? » What is the first step in the business process? » What occurs prior to this first step? (This will help later when you move to step 3 and map the existing process.) » Where does the business process end? » What is the last activity included in the process?	
☐ Process Responsibilities: What does the business process have responsibility to deliver?	

QUESTION	ANSWER

☐ Customer and Needs:
  » Who is the customer of this process?
  » Who is the end user of the process - the individual who buys the product or service? If you work with internal clients, this could be who funds the work (or has budgetary responsibility).
  » What does the customer care about relative to this process?
  » What will they pay for?
  » What value do they want?	

☐ Key Stakeholders and Needs:
  » What other departments are affected by this business process?
  » What other departments receive the downstream effect of the process?
  » What do they care about? What is their interest in the process?	

☐ Measurements of Success:
  » What does success look like?
  » How will we know if the process is successful?
  » Did we cover the customer and stakeholder needs?
  » Are there any internal measurements that we should include to make sure that the business remains efficient in delivering the results?	

STEP 3: PROCESS MAP

QUESTION	ANSWER
☐ Referring back to the scope definition document, review the "scope" section and ask questions such as: » Okay, since we defined <_what you wrote_> as the first step in the process, what happens now? » Who has responsibility to <_what you wrote_> (from activity one)? » What happens next? Depending on the activity description and who performed the activity, you can ask something like "You've gotten a call from a manager who wants to <_what you wrote_>, what happens next?" » If you receive multiple answers (or hear people say, "Well, it all depends"), draw a decision symbol. » Before moving to activity two ask, "What is the output of activity one," or "What do you have now that <_what you wrote_> has occurred?"	
☐ For activity two, build off what you wrote as the output for activity one by asking,: » Now that we have <_activity one output_>, what happens to it? Focus on what happens to the output to decide what to write in the activity two box. » If you have trouble getting an answer, ask more precise questions like, "Who is the <_output_> sent to (or used by), how is it sent, and what do they do with it?"	

Continue asking the same questions activity by activity. Reword your questions based on the output of each activity, since the output of one activity must provide the input to the next activity.

Step 4: Estimate Time and Cost

Referring back to each activity on the process map, use these questions to identify the process and cycle times. Feel free to write ranges on the process map, for example, 5-10 minutes.

Question	Answer
☐ Process time: » How long does it take for the manager (or other person responsible) to perform this task? » If you have pushback ask, "How long would it take *you* to complete this task?" » If you still have pushback ask someone to research the answer and come back to the project team.	
☐ Cycle time: » How long will this activity take considering waiting time, interruptions, or other delays that may occur? » We know that it takes the manager (or other person responsible) in activity one about <*the amount of time previously defined*, e.g., 20 minutes> to <*task*>, but I want you to think now about interruptions that the manager may have or additional tasks, unrelated to <*task*> that the manager may have to handle before finishing the <*task*>. The phone may ring, a colleague may walk into the office, or his or her boss may request something unexpectedly. With all these interruptions, how long do you estimate it takes to finish the <*task*>?	

QUESTION	ANSWER
☐ Process cost: Add up the process time consumed by a business process to calculate the cost. » What is the annual volume handled? For example, "How many rewards are processed in a year?" "How many product inquiries do we handle in a year?" » What departments have a major role in the business process? » What departments should we include in the cost calculation? » Who does the work in the department(s) and what is the affected employees' annual salary? » What FTE formula will we use? » What is the employee benefit rate to use? » Should we apply tool and overhead costs? What rate will we use?	

STEP 5: VERIFY PROCESS MAP

QUESTION	ANSWER
☐ What stakeholders and process workers should we include in the validation step?	
☐ After reviewing the scope definition document and process map, ask each stakeholder or process worker: » Do you agree with the accuracy of the process map? » Are there any points requiring clarification from your perspective? » Do you agree with the time estimates on the process map? » Do you see anything major missing?	

Step 6: Apply Improvement Techniques

As you apply the improvement techniques, you will start uncovering cultural changes that have to occur in the organization, and these types of changes are often difficult to implement. Nevertheless, keep track of them, even though they may take a long time to accomplish.

Use the impact analysis as a tool to capture changes that need to occur to implement a new, improved business process. Do not exclude a change from your plans just because it appears challenging. Sometimes you exact the biggest gains from difficult changes.

Question	Answer
Bureaucracy If an activity does not contribute to customer satisfaction, if it negatively affects cycle time, or if it increases cost, eliminate it.	
☐ How many approvals do we have in place? Why?	
☐ How can we reduce the number of approvals required?	
☐ Do we make decisions at the right point in the process?	
☐ Do we generate unnecessary paperwork?	

Question	Answer
☐ What forms can we eliminate? If you receive pushback on eliminating forms, ask, "Why do we need them?"	
☐ How many copies of each document do we make?	
☐ Why do we keep hardcopies?	
☐ Do we understand what people do with the information or reports that we send them?	
☐ Do people receive information that they do not need (or no longer require)?	
☐ Does one person check the work of another? Why?	
☐ How do individuals use the information requested on a form in making decisions?	

QUESTION	ANSWER
☐ Do we have unnecessary rules?	
☐ Does a policy or procedure get in the way?	
☐ What will happen if an employee makes a mistake? Does the added scrutiny seem worth the expense?	
☐ Does the activity support a SALT (statutory, audit, legal, or tax) requirement?	
☐ Why, why, why, why, why?	

QUESTION	ANSWER
Value Added The hardest activities to eliminate are those that the business considers valuable for their own reasons because the temptation to say an activity adds business value, instead of being a bureaucratic step, is far too easy. Think strategically, keep the big picture in mind, and show courage by challenging business value added activities.	
☐ What value does this activity contribute? To who?	
☐ Does the activity contribute to customer value added or business value added?	
☐ Why does the customer care about this activity?	
☐ Would the customer pay for this activity if they knew it existed?	

QUESTION	ANSWER
Duplication You may have to talk to other departments to uncover redundancy if your process map focuses only on one department. Find out what happens at the other end of an activity after you hand something off to another department.	
☐ Is there a single source of data?	
☐ Does more than one employee do the same work? Are two employees generating similar reports?	
☐ How many employees maintain the same data?	
☐ Where do we see dual entry of information? How can we eliminate the dual entry?	
☐ How can we minimize duplicate document storage? How clear is the file naming convention?	

QUESTION	ANSWER
☐ What programs have similar goals, strategies, or activities?	
☐ What programs target similar end users?	
☐ Are two or more departments performing similar services for the same audience?	

Simplification

Simplification, or streamlining the process, means reducing or eliminating the complexity of a business process so that the process becomes easier to understand and more efficient. When you keep a process simple, it becomes easier to sustain and more flexible in responding to customer needs.

☐ What steps can we streamline in the process?	
☐ What forms can we streamline or simplify? What unnecessary information resides on the form?	

QUESTION	ANSWER
☐ What questions do employees have when completing a form?	
☐ Where do employees have to go to obtain the information required on the form?	
☐ How many emails are sent at any point in the process? A substantial number of emails signals that unnecessary complexity exists.	
☐ Where do employees go to obtain information to complete any step in the process?	
☐ What roadblocks do we see?	
☐ What unnecessary handoffs do we see?	
☐ How can we standardize a step, a report, or a form to make it easier to understand?	

QUESTION	ANSWER
☐ Do we know the number of errors made and why?	
☐ What steps in the process can we eliminate or combine with others?	
☐ Must process workers call other people to complete any step in the process? Why?	
☐ Does everyone understand the process?	
☐ How does the organization use the data and reports throughout the process?	
Cycle Time Customers care about cycle time because they experience it in the form of delays.	
☐ Why do delays occur?	

Question	Answer
☐ Where do handoffs occur? How can we reduce handoffs?	
☐ Where can we reduce the waiting time that occurs between activities in the process?	
☐ Where can we optimize activities that add value to the process?	
☐ What activities can we eliminate that do not add value and that have a long cycle time?	
☐ What activities can we perform in parallel instead of one at a time?	
☐ What activities can we combine?	
☐ What industry standards should we benchmark?	

QUESTION	ANSWER
☐ Where can we change the sequence of activities to make the process more efficient?	
☐ Where can we speed up an activity without diminishing the quality?	
☐ Where can we reduce interruptions?	

Automation

As you move through the improvement techniques, remember that:
- "Automation applied to an efficient operation will magnify the efficiency."
- "Automation applied to an inefficient operation will magnify the inefficiency."

☐ What desktop tools do we have available today?	
☐ What collaboration tools are available?	
☐ What enterprise systems exist? ☐ What is the upgrade schedule for the enterprise systems?	

Question	Answer
☐ What is the process for scheduling improvements to enterprise or departmental systems?	

Step 7: Create Internal Controls, Tools, and Metrics

Question	Answer
☐ What can go wrong at this point (asking at each activity on the **new** process map)?	
☐ What mistakes can occur?	
☐ What can an employee do wrong at this step in the process?	
☐ What specific issues can occur?	
☐ What can we do to avoid the potential error?	
☐ What *measurements of success* (from the scope definition document) should we develop metrics for to begin?	
☐ How can we measure <*a single measurement of success*>? For example, how can we measure "quality?"	

QUESTION	ANSWER
☐ What does success look like?	
☐ What baseline will we use for each metric?	
☐ Do we have a mix of metrics that address effectiveness, efficiency, and adaptability?	

STEP 8: TEST AND REWORK

QUESTION	ANSWER
☐ What do we want to test?	
☐ What different scenarios should we test?	
☐ Who should we involve in the testing?	
☐ Where should the testing occur?	
☐ When should we conduct the testing? Are there any time periods that we should avoid due to high business demand?	

Step 9: Implement the Change

Question	Answer
☐ Training: » Who requires the training? » Who owns the responsibility to conduct the training? » What topics do the participants have to know? » Where should we conduct the training? » When should we train? » What methods will we use to conduct the training?	
☐ Communications: » What is the purpose for the communication (the goal)? » What does each audience group have to know about the change (key message points)? » How will we communicate with each audience (communication vehicles or the how)? » When will we communicate with each audience (timing)?	
☐ Impact Analysis: » Who will handle each of the issues identified in the analysis? » What is the escalation process if consensus cannot be gained?	

Step 10: Continuous Improvement

Question	Answer
☐ Does the process continue to deliver the effectiveness, efficiency, and adaptability (or flexibility) intended?	
☐ What bottlenecks exist?	
☐ Does the process deliver what the scope definition document identified as customer needs?	
☐ How have customer needs changed?	
☐ Do the process workers follow the documented process? Why not?	
☐ Do the stakeholders receive what they require from the business process?	
☐ Do the third parties deliver what they said they would deliver?	
☐ What new internal controls should the organization add to help eliminate errors?	
☐ What new responsibilities has the process assumed?	

QUESTION	ANSWER
☐ How can the organization better train new employees?	
☐ How can we make the communication process more effective?	
☐ How can employees more easily share information and knowledge?	
☐ Continuous Improvement Plan: » How often should we review the main activities (measurement data, revisit customer needs, test internal controls, validate that process workers follow the process, revisit stakeholder needs, and evaluate third-party performance)? » What data source will we use for each activity? » How will we conduct the evaluation (method to use)? » Who will conduct the evaluation?	

Building Consensus

How to build consensus is a common concern and it requires you to have patience and facilitation skills.

DEFINITION: Consensus means "majority of opinion" or "general agreement," but does this mean that all parties agree one hundred percent? No, consensus is not a vote. It means that adequate discussion has occurred and that all parties can support the decision or approach.

If you follow the ten steps to business process improvement, in the order presented, you will find a natural progression to consensus building because each step builds on the previous step and each step increases the project team's investment in the work. Investment leads to consensus.

Creating the scope definition document (step 2) together as a project team starts the journey. As the facilitator, you must move slowly through the development of this document to allow all participants an opportunity to express his or her opinion. Discussing this foundational information with the project team at the start of the first meeting allows everyone to have input and assists the team in coming to a common understanding of the business process and terminology. If a participant does not speak during this step, you must engage the person. The scope definition document not only provides you with a blueprint moving forward, but also provides a pseudo contract. The successful completion of the scope definition document demonstrates your ability to facilitate a group.

Drawing the current state process map (step 3) continues to engage the project team. It helps everyone involved in creating the process map learn how the process works, what activities constitute most of the work, where the handoffs occur between departments, and where the opportunities for improvement exist.

As the facilitator, you have to elicit the information out of the team, rather than supplying the answers. In your role as facilitator, you should never give the answer, but you may need to rephrase comments made by the project team, so that you write clear and concise statements on the process map.

As you draw the process map over several meetings, revisit the previous meeting's work, so that all participants remember where the team left off at the last meeting. Make any necessary changes to the existing work before proceeding to finish drawing the process map. This again allows everyone to feel engaged and listened to, another step towards building consensus.

Estimating the process and cycle times (step 4) further draws the project team in and makes them feel more invested in the process work, and including the team in the verification step (step 5) causes the participants to represent the work with other employees in the organization - a key strategy to encourage ownership of the process. You should have consensus of the current state before beginning step 6 (applying improvement techniques), or you will have a difficult time leading the project team through this step.

Facilitation Tips

You may find it difficult to lead a project team through business process improvement, especially if the participants do not want to attend or participate in the effort. Do you have a willing team of volunteers or has management drafted employees to join the team?

Today, employees want to know "What's in it for me?" Follow these tips to provide good facilitation and engage a project team:

- Be prepared and on time
- Know your audience
- Create a safe environment

- Summarize discussions
- Ask open-ended questions
- Make eye contact with everyone
- Remain neutral and help the group come to conclusions
- Keep a pulse on all participants (remember the quiet ones)
- Manage conflicts (know the difference between a debate and an argument)
- Know when to move on
- Make it clear when you offer "expert" advice (vs. facilitating)

Learning the Material

One of the easiest ways to learn how to use each of the ten steps is to practice with a topic that you already know. Consider a major purchase you plan to make this year - perhaps a vacation or a home improvement project.

Use the prioritization matrix in Figure 1-7 to identify the criteria you will use to make a decision on where to go on vacation or the best home improvement project. You will learn how to define categories, apply a scale, and whether to weigh the criteria. This exercise will demonstrate the simplicity of the matrix and help you to feel comfortable using it in a business environment.

Next, create a scope definition document, using Figure 2-10, for the major purchase you chose and adapt the template to address your personal project. As you draft the document, talk to a family member as practice for working with a project team.

Then you can outline the steps involved in your project in a process flow format using the techniques from step 3. If you have software available, transfer your paper process map to an electronic version.

Now that you have the steps of your project outlined, estimate how long it will take to accomplish each step (the process time) and how much it will cost. Review the process map and estimates with the family member as practice for step 5.

For step 6, you will probably find it easier to use an everyday process such as "getting out of the house in the morning." How can you improve your morning routine (or your personal process) so that you reduce your prep time in the morning by twenty percent?

Most of the steps involve common sense and you should have an easy time trying them out in a non-threatening situation.

Templates

The following pages include the most common templates you will use. For copies of all the templates used in this workbook, visit: www.susanpagebooks.com. Use the authorization code on page one to access a special section of the web site.

Process Prioritization Matrix

Process Name/Category											Total Score
Sub-category											
1.											
2.											
3.											
4.											
5.											
6.											
7.											
8.											
9.											
10.											
11.											
12.											

Process Prioritization Matrix

Process Name/Category									Total Score
Sub-category									
1.									
2.									
3.									
4.									
5.									
6.									
7.									
8.									
9.									
10.									
11.									
12.									

Process Prioritization Matrix

Scope Definition

Process Name: _____

Process Owner: _____

Description (Purpose)

Scope (Boundaries):

Start: _____

End: _____

Process Responsibilities:

- ■ ■ ■ ■ ■ ■ ■

Customer/Client: _____

Customer/Client Needs:

- ■ ■ ■ ■ ■

Key Stakeholders & Interest:

Measurements of Success:

1.
2.
3.
4.
5.

Scope Definition

Process Name: _____

Process Owner: _____

Customer/Client: _____

Description (Purpose)

Customer/Client Needs:

- ■
- ■
- ■
- ■
- ■

Key Stakeholders & Interest:

Scope (Boundaries):

Start: _____

End: _____

Measurements of Success:

1.
2.
3.
4.
5.

Process Responsibilities:

- ■
- ■
- ■
- ■
- ■
- ■

Process Name _____

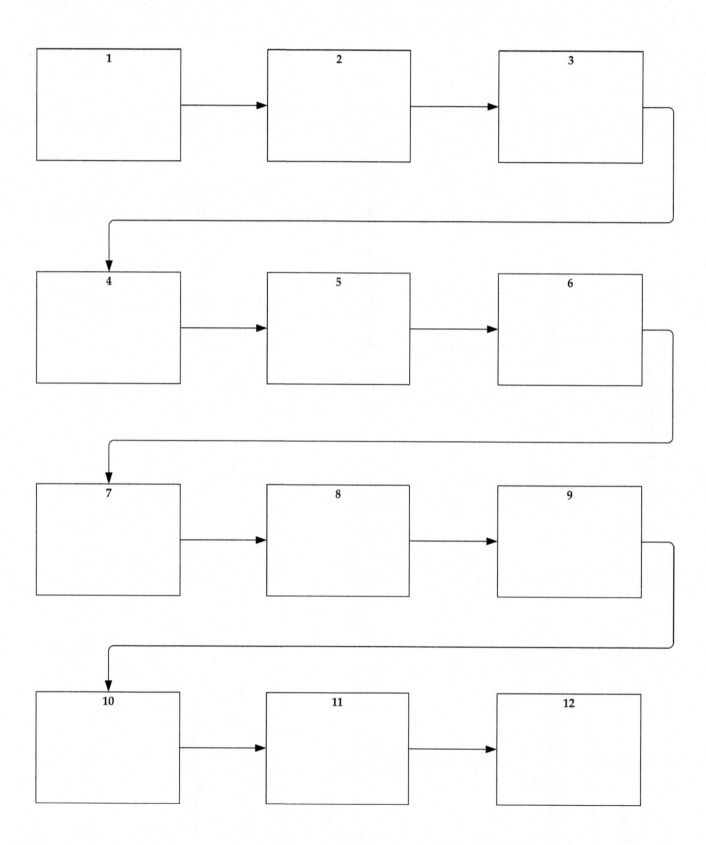

Process Name _____

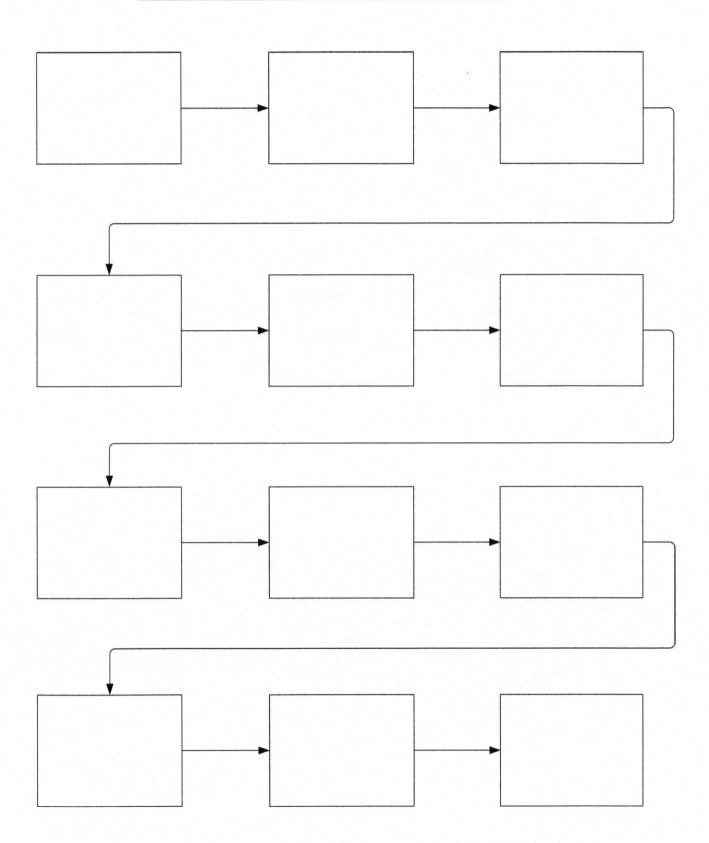

SUSAN PAGE is an experienced business process improvement consultant who has worked with the computer, banking,  health management, and entertainment industries. She is the author of the popular book on improving a company's business processes. *The Power of Business Process Improvement*, published by the American Management Association, has become an industry standard for anyone new to business process improvement, and a tool for others. She has worked for a major entertainment company in Orlando, Florida, for the past 16 years, and is currently a manager of Human Resources Information Systems (HRIS).

CPSIA information can be obtained
at www.ICGtesting.com
Printed in the USA
LVOW02s0251220116

471830LV00018B/464/P